W9-BBH-233

Spain
and the
Roanoke Voyages

This chart of the Atlantic Ocean and the east coast of North America is from "Queen Mary's Atlas" (1558), by Diogo Homem. Spanish claims, as represented by the banner and royal arms shown left of center, extend up the east coast to the mouth of the St. Lawrence River. The Spanish referred to the entire North American continent as "Terra de Florida." Map reproduced courtesy the British Library Board, London, England.

Spain
and the
Roanoke Voyages

by
Paul E. Hoffman

Raleigh
America's Four Hundredth Anniversary Committee
North Carolina Department of Cultural Resources
1987

America's Four Hundredth Anniversary Committee

Lindsay C. Warren, Jr.
Chairman

Contents

Maps and Illustrations

Foreword

America's Four Hundredth Anniversary Committee, formed in 1978 under the provisions of an act of the North Carolina General Assembly of 1973, was charged with recommending plans for the observance of the quadricentennial of the first English attempts to explore and settle North America. The committee has proposed to carry out a variety of programs to appeal to a broad range of people. Among these is a publications program that includes a series of booklets dealing with the history of the events and people of the 1580s.

Queen Elizabeth I of England enjoyed a reign that was for the most part peaceful. It was a period of prosperity, which saw the flourishing of a new interest in literature, religion, exploration, and business. English mariners began to venture farther from home, and in time talk began to be heard of hopes to establish naval bases and colonies in America. Men of the County of Devon in the southwest of England, seafarers for generations, played leading roles in this expansion. One of these, Walter Ralegh (as he most often wrote his name), became a favorite of the queen, and on him she bestowed a variety of honors and rewards. It was he to whom she granted a charter in 1584 authorizing the discovery and occupation of lands not already held by "any Christian Prince and . . . people." Ralegh promptly sent a reconnaissance expedition to what is now North Carolina, and this was followed in due time by a colony under the leadership of Ralph Lane. Headquarters were established on Roanoke Island. After remaining for nearly a year and exploring far afield, Lane and his men returned to England in 1586.

In the summer of 1587 Governor John White and a colony of 115 men, women, and children arrived and occupied the houses and the fort left by Lane. The brief annals of this colony are recorded in a journal kept by the governor; they tell of certain problems that arose early—but they also record the birth of the first English child in America. The journal further explains why Governor White consented to return to England for supplies. His departure was the last contact

ix

with the settlers who constituted the "Lost Colony," renowned in history, literature, and folklore.

Although a casual acquaintance with the facts of these English efforts might suggest that they were failures, such was far from the case. Ralegh's expenditures of time, effort, and resources (in which he was joined by many others, including Queen Elizabeth herself) had salutary effects for England and certainly for all of present-day America. From Ralegh's initial investment in the reconnaissance voyage, as well as from the colonies, came careful descriptions of the New World and samples of its products. The people of England, indeed of the Western world, learned about North America; because books were published based on what Ralegh's men discovered, they could soon read for themselves of the natives there and the promise of strange and wonderful new resources.

From these voyages and colonizing efforts came the conviction that an English nation could be established in America. In 1606, when another charter was about to be issued for further settlement, King James, who succeeded Queen Elizabeth at her death in 1603, called for advice from some of the men who had been associated with Ralegh. They assured the king that further efforts would surely succeed. With this the Virginia Company was chartered, and it established England's first permanent settlement in America at Jamestown.

Because of Sir Walter Ralegh's vision, England persisted. Because of England's persistence and its refusal to yield to Spain's claims to the region, the United States today enjoys an English heritage. The English common law is the basis of American law; American legislative bodies are modeled on the House of Commons with the rights and freedoms that it developed over a long period of time; America's mother tongue is English, and it is the most commonly spoken language in the world—pilots and navigators on international airlines and the controllers who direct them at airports all over the world use English. Americans also share England's literary tradition: Chaucer, Beowulf, King Arthur, and Shakespeare are America's too, and Americans can enjoy Dickens and Tennyson, as well as Agatha Christie and Dorothy Sayers. America's religious freedom is also in the English tradition, and several of this nation's Protestant denominations trace their earliest history to origins in England: the Episcopal church, certainly, but the Quakers, Baptists, Congregationalists, and Universalists as well.

America's Four Hundredth Anniversary Committee has planned many programs to direct national and even international attention to the significance of events that occurred from bases established by English men, women, and children, but notably Sir Walter Ralegh, in what is now North Carolina during the period 1584-1590. While some of the programs may be regarded as fleeting and soon forgotten, the publications are intended to serve as lasting reminders of America's indebtedness to England. Books, pamphlets, and folders covering a broad range of topics have been prepared by authors on both sides of the Atlantic. These, it is anticipated, will introduce a vast new audience to the facts of America's origins.

Lindsay C. Warren, Jr., *Chairman*
America's Four Hundredth Anniversary Committee

Introduction

This study presupposes that the reader will also be studying the other booklets in this series, particularly David Beers Quinn's *The Lost Colonists: Their Fortune and Probable Fate.* There the reader will discover what actually happened during the Roanoke voyages as the participants knew the story and as the foremost modern scholar of the voyage has been able to reconstruct it from English, Spanish, and other sources. This booklet reports what the Spanish understood and did about those voyages. Consequently, as reported here, some facts about the English voyages are not accurate because the Spanish did not know the entire story.

Besides reporting what the Spanish understood and did about the Roanoke voyages, this study attempts to account for why they did not do or try to do more, or do it sooner than they did. At some points in the story the reasons are clear and well documented, but at others a lack of documentation creates uncertainty about why the Spanish acted in certain ways. Thus, this study points to work still to be done in understanding the Spanish side of the Roanoke story.

I. European Voyages to the Outer Banks Prior to 1584

At the time Sir Walter Ralegh and his friends decided to found a colony in the New World, there existed a body of information about the areas that interested them. This information derived from the voyages of many Europeans, especially the Spanish. At once specific on some points and vague on many others, it was supported by prevailing geographic theory, which held that at similar latitudes north and south of the equator similar climates and resources, especially mineral resources, would be found. It was thus possible to project onto the geography of the New World a variety of hopes and wishes concerning what might be possible if a colony were created at a particular latitude. The Outer Banks lay in an area in which both geographic theory and actual knowledge gained from prior voyages suggested the viability of a colony that would satisfy the desires of many interests in Elizabethan England. Pre-1584 voyages north of Cape Hatteras by the Spanish suggested opposite, pessimistic conclusions about the area where rumor and report had it that the English had settled. Consequently, the Spanish search for the English was less vigorous than it might have been had the former valued more highly the area in question.

The first documented European voyage along the coast of what became North Carolina was in 1524, but Europeans probably saw the coast before that date. The discovery of Bermuda in 1505 and the pre-1520 cartography that shows Cuba as an island and the Bahama Islands in their correct position relative to the Greater Antilles suggest as much.

The voyage of 1524 was led by the Florentine Giovanni da Verrazzano, who sailed along the coast in the service of Francis I, king of France, and of a group of Italian merchants resident in Lyon. In common with a number of Spanish explorers of his time, Verrazzano was seeking a westward passage to the Orient via an American strait. He knew about the Spanish discoveries of Florida and may have known about the closed nature of the Gulf of Mexico as well as about New-foundland and Nova Scotia. Because of the absence of geographical knowledge concerning the middle latitudes of North America, that area may have been viewed as a possible open-water passage to the Orient. Academic geographers, whose ideas were known to Verrazzano, said that such a passage had to exist.

Verrazzano made his landfall at about the place where the present border between North Carolina and South Carolina meets the sea, at a latitude he reported as 34 degrees north. From there he sailed to the south, possibly as far as the southern part of present-day Georgia. He then turned back to the north, returning to the Carolina coast. After anchoring near his original landfall to make contact with the Indians and attempting to go ashore near Cape Lookout, Verrazzano sailed north along the shore, just off what he described in one manuscript account as "an isthmus one mile wide and about two hundred miles long, in which we could see the eastern sea from the ship, halfway between west and north." He continued by reporting that "This is doubtless the one which goes around the tip of India, China, and Cathay. We sailed along this isthmus, hoping all the time to find some strait or real promontory where the land might end to the north, and we could reach those blessed shores of Cathay. This isthmus was named by the discoverer 'Varazanio,' just as all the land we found was called 'Francesca' after our Francis [I, king of France]."[1] From his "isthmus" Verrazzano sailed on to the north, visiting the

In 1524 Giovanni da Verrazzano led the first documented European voyage along the coast of what later became North Carolina. The Florentine explorer, like many of his Spanish counterparts, sought a westward passage to the Orient by way of a strait that was believed to exist in the middle latitudes of North America. Engraving from John Fiske, *The Dutch and Quaker Colonies in America* (Boston and New York: Houghton, Mifflin and Company, 2 volumes, 1903), I, facing p. 54.

Delmarva peninsula and New York harbor, among other places, before returning to France.

The "isthmus" was the Outer Banks, the long series of barrier islands that extend from Cape Lookout to near Cape Henry, Virginia. The "eastern sea" was the waters of Albemarle and Pamlico sounds glimpsed from the masthead of the ship in places where the sand dunes were not covered by forests too high or too dense to allow a view of the water behind the islands. Why Verrazzano did not see one or more of the inlets that undoubtedly existed then (but which have since shifted) is a mystery that has puzzled scholars ever since.

Whatever Verrazzano's reasons for failing to find a way through the "isthmus," the concept of such a land formation at about 35 degrees to 37 degrees north latitude became a part of the cartography of some of the map makers from Dieppe, the French Atlantic seaport from which many later French explorers and commerce raiders set out and with which the English had commercial and other ties of long standing. A generation later, Pedro Menéndez de Avilés, the founder of the permanent Spanish colony in Florida, convinced himself that a portage from Chesapeake Bay would quickly carry a traveler to the arm of the Pacific that lay to the west. Sir Walter Ralegh and his agents may have held a similar view of the possibility of using Verrazzano's "isthmus" as a means of reaching the portion of the South Sea that academic geographers of his time still believed existed in North America.

A year after Verrazzano's voyage, the Spanish pilot Pedro de Quejo also coasted the area of the Outer Banks, but with greater care and attention to the inlets between Cape Hatteras and Cape Henry. The result was a cartographic tradition and an oral tradition about the area that served to discourage further Spanish interest in it. Quejo was in the employ of the Licenciado Lucas Vázquez de Ayllón, a judge on the appeals court (*Audiencia*) at Santo Domingo, presently the capital city of the Dominican Republic but then the administrative center for much of the Spanish Caribbean. Following up on a discovery made by Quejo in 1521 at 33 degrees 20 minutes north latitude (the present area of Winyah Bay, South Carolina), Ayllón in 1523 obtained a contract for exploration and settlement and dispatched Quejo to explore North America in the hope that he might find a strait.

Quejo's course along the North American coast in 1525 is known from a few comments made by Ayllón during the course of a lawsuit

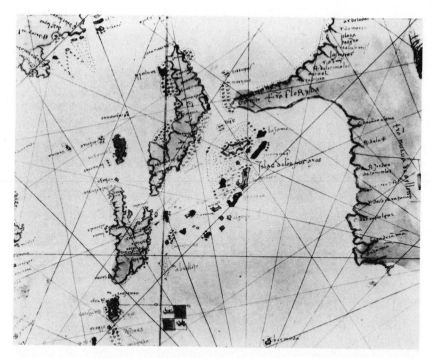

This portion of Juan Vespucci's 1526 map of the world shows the eastern coast of North America and the Caribbean area. The map includes new information gained by the Spanish pilot Pedro de Quejo during a voyage along the North American coast in 1525. Map from the files of the Division of Archives and History.

over who had the right to the discovery (a suit brought against Ayllón by one of his partners in the exploration of 1521), from the Juan Vespucci map of 1526, and from sailing directions (rutter) compiled in Seville and known from the manuscript (ca. 1539) of Alonso de Chaves. No narrative has been preserved, although some of Chaves's material was probably copied from Quejo's original report.

These sources demonstrate that Quejo sailed along the Outer Banks, perhaps from north to south, and entered two inlets north of Cape Hatteras and another about fifty nautical miles to the south. The northernmost inlet gave access to a bay that Chaves's materials indicate was named Bahia de Santa Maria (Saint Mary's Bay) because it was apparently entered on July 2, the date of the festival of the Visitation of the Virgin Mary in the Spanish calendar of saints. By overlaying the data from Chaves on a modern map, it can be shown that the inlet is in approximately the same position as an unnamed inlet mapped by the English in 1585. The second inlet is unnamed

4

in the Chaves manuscript but corresponds to Trinity harbor on the English maps of 1585-1587. The southernmost inlet, named River of the Prince in the Chaves material (in honor of the future Philip II, who was born in 1527), is also shown on the English maps, but without a name. Quejo thus explored the Outer Banks and found entrances into Albemarle and Pamlico sounds.

During this same voyage Quejo explored Chesapeake Bay, shown on the Vespucci map as a large, circular bay well to the north of the three entrances just discussed. On the map, the name Bahia de Santa Maria is written so that it appears to correspond to this feature rather than to the entrance to the south, where Chaves's material places that name. Probably for that reason, the name Bahia de Santa Maria was attached to the Chesapeake when the official map of the coast was drawn in 1527 by Diego de Rivero, Chaves's predecessor in the office of cosmographer. The Rivero map also shows Chesapeake Bay as having three small islands in its mouth, features accurate for the Outer Banks area but not for the Chesapeake. The coastal outline Quejo's voyage supplied was quickly altered in ways that confused not only the names he had used but also the geographic features to which they related.

It is not known what Quejo reported about the appearance and resources of either the Outer Banks or Chesapeake Bay. It is known that when Ayllón came to the coast in 1526 to found a settlement, he chose to go to the area explored in 1521 rather than to the higher latitudes specified in his 1523 contract and explored by Quejo, even though those latitudes, 35 degrees to 37 degrees north, had been specified because of his claim that his men had discovered a land at the same latitude as Andalusia, Spain's southernmost region, which is centered about 37 degrees north. Such a claim was good propaganda and bespeaks Quejo's belief, and that of his audience in Spain, that at similar latitudes similar climates were to be found, meaning that soils and floral resources were similar and that the area could be expected to produce the crops for which Andalusia has been famous since Roman times: wine grapes and olives. Peter Martyr, Ayllón's contemporary and host during the latter's stay in Spain in 1523, said that this is what Ayllón was telling everyone at court.

Ayllón's failure to attempt settlement in the area of North Carolina and southern Virginia and the lack of resources he found when the colony actually landed in the Santee River-Winyah Bay area and attempted to set up a camp gave the entire coast from Winyah Bay north a bad name among the Spanish. Alonso de Santa Cruz, the official Spanish cosmographer during the 1540s and 1550s, described the coast as a group of useless "desert" islands of sand. The term "desert" suggested not only the islands' lack of natural resources but also the absence of inhabitants. Both were essential to the sort of imperialism the Spanish customarily practiced in the New World, whether carried out by military conquest, as in Mexico and Peru, or by the establishment of missions, as in New Mexico and Paraguay.

Having written off the Atlantic coast of North America as useless for their colonial purposes, the Spanish did not return to it until the 1560s and then primarily to prevent its occupation by subjects of the French king. French settlement anywhere along the coast south of Newfoundland challenged the Spanish claim based upon prior discovery and attempted settlement and seemed to some Spaniards to pose a danger to the movement of the Spanish treasure fleets through the Bahama Channel on the way from Havana to Spain.

On this reverse of a Spanish silver medal, cast and chased ca. 1560, a native South American woman representing the Indies ("INDIA") is shown presenting the abundance ("RELIQUUM") of the New World to Spain. Note the galleons visible in the background. Photograph courtesy Trustees of the British Museum, London, England.

The object of most of this concern was what the Spaniards had come to believe was the area of Ayllón's discovery of 1521: the "Point of Santa Elena" (present-day Tybee Island) and the "Jordan River." The French, too, believed that this combination of geographic features would help them identify the location of Ayllón's discovery, the supposed riches of which they knew about from reading Peter Martyr's account, an extravagantly phrased promotional story that Ayllón had spread in Spain in 1523. Both the French and the Spanish thought they knew where these places were—at 32 degrees north, where Francisco Lopez de Gómara had located them in his *General History of the Indies,* first published in 1552. Martyr's account, which had been published in 1530, suggested that the Jordan River would provide a large harbor and offer access to a land rich in resources and populated by Indians. In short, the Jordan was the ideal site for a French colony of settlement and for a naval base that could be used to threaten Spanish colonies and shipping in the Caribbean.

Spanish concerns about French designs on the Point of Santa Elena grew more intense during the 1550s. To prevent French occupation there, Spanish explorer, soldier, and administrator Tristan de Luna was sent from Mexico to settle on the Gulf Coast and then establish a colony at the Point of Santa Elena. At the same time, Spanish diplomats in Europe attempted to induce the French to agree to a delimitation of the Spanish Indies that would include enough of the North American continent and the Atlantic Ocean off its coasts to protect Spanish shipping from the French commerce raiding that had become commonplace since the 1530s, even during peacetime. When this diplomatic effort failed, as it clearly had by December, 1559, Philip II of Spain ordered that Luna or someone he might send proceed at once to occupy the Point of Santa Elena and the harbor believed to be near it. At the time, Luna's colony was barely surviving in camps near present-day Pensacola, Florida, and Gadsden, Alabama.

The result of Philip's order was the voyage of Angel de Villafañe in the spring of 1561. Villafañe, formerly a soldier in Mexico and

This engraving of Philip II, king of Spain, was rendered in 1586, when the monarch was fifty-nine years old. He assumed the Spanish throne in 1556 on the abdication of his father, Charles V. Engraving courtesy Trustees of the British Museum.

7

a judicial officer in Mexico City, sailed from Havana to a point near present-day Port Royal Sound. Exploring a river that he reported was the River of Santa Elena but finding that it had a shallow entrance and offered nothing useful for colonization, he left the area and went up the coast in search of the Jordan River. Unlike the French under Jean Ribault, who were to explore the same area the following spring, Villafañe seems to have known that the Point of Santa Elena and the Jordan River were separated by a number of degrees of latitude. Consequently, he went to Cape Fear, the first cape he found along the coast that had a large river to the west. According to the chart he carried, the Jordan River had a cape northeast of it. Cape Fear, and the Cape Fear River, seemed to match the chart. He thus passed by the entrance to the Santee River and Winyah Bay, the actual location of Ayllón's Jordan River.

Villafañe set out to sail northward along the coast to see what other rivers and capes he could find. It is not known how far he got, but he may have been off Cape Hatteras when a storm scattered his fleet, sinking one ship and forcing him to take a course to the southeast, which eventually carried him to Monte Cristi on the northern coast of what is now the Dominican Republic. There he drew up a report recounting his voyage and saying that neither the River of Santa Elena nor the Jordan River, as he understood them, was suitable for settlement. Duly forwarded to Spain, this opinion was taken at face value, and fears of a French colony at either place were put aside. Once again the coast at the mid-30s north latitude was dismissed by the Spanish as of no value for settlement.

As Villafañe's report was being received in Spain, Jean Ribault was sailing for North America. Landing first just south of the St. Johns River in Florida, he worked his way up the coast until he came to the bay he named Port Royal. As both he and his contemporary, René de Laudonnière, related the story, he believed that he had reached the Jordan River and the location of "Chicora," a town on the Jordan that had figured in Peter Martyr's account of the Ayllón discovery. Believing the promise of Martyr's tale about rich resources and needing to reduce the size of his crews because of a shortage of supplies, Ribault persuaded thirty of his men to remain in a small fort he built at present-day Parris Island on a stream flowing into the Beaufort River, one of the two principal arms of Port Royal Sound. Ribault then sailed to Europe, believing he would be able to return the following spring with additional men and supplies.

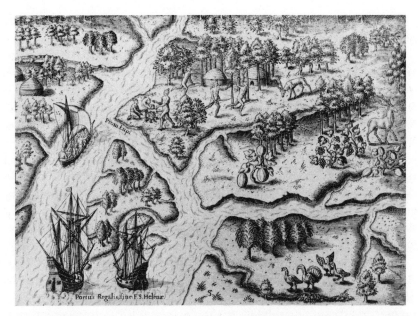

As a means of ensuring control of Florida, the Spanish maintained a fort on Santa Elena (present-day Parris Island, South Carolina). This engraving shows a portion of the island in 1562, at which time the French (whose ships are shown in the left foreground) attempted to plant a settlement there. Engraving by Jacques le Moyne de Morgues; from Theodor de Bry's *America* (1591), part 2, plate V. Reproduced courtesy the British Library Board.

Upon returning to European waters, Ribault was captured by the English and forced to spend the winter of 1562-1563 in London. There he composed a report in English and had a version of it printed. This was the only original, firsthand information about the North American coast to be printed in England up to that time. It was also the first account of the coast by a non-Spaniard since the publication of Verrazzano's narrative in Italy in 1556. English interest in North American rather than Caribbean colonization may well date from this report.

An unintended consequence of Villafañe's voyage was the voyage of Antonio de Velázquez. Given command of a supply vessel by Villafañe with orders to follow him northward, Velázquez was carrying out his instructions when he was blown off course by a storm and carried by the current of the Gulf Stream well to the north of Cape Hatteras. His account of the voyage has not been found, but from fragmentary evidence it appears that his ship put into Chesapeake Bay after the storm had abated. There he encountered two Indians, who agreed to travel with the Europeans aboard their ship. They arrived in Seville in September, 1561.

Information obtained by the Spanish from the Indians concerning their homeland, as well as what Velázquez had seen, caused a wave of excitement and renewed interest in the North American coast north of the Point of Santa Elena. Especially interested in this report was Lucas Vázquez de Ayllón, the younger, son of the man who had attempted to found a colony in North America in 1526.

Ayllón, the younger, soon went to court to press a claim to the new discovery, and indeed to all of the Atlantic coast below about 37 degrees north latitude. By then in his fifties, Ayllón was moderately successful in commerce and was married to a woman much his junior who had some inheritance. Moreover, he had claim to his father's estates on the northern coast of Española. He now offered to establish a mission and small agricultural colony at some point on the North American coast described only as "the port of Florida." In February, 1562, Philip II agreed, undoubtedly because at about that same time he learned from his ambassador in Paris that Ribault was planning a colony on the coast of North America, or "Florida," as both he and the Spanish called it.

Because of difficulties in raising money, recruiting and clearing colonists through the emigration regulations of the House of Trade (only persons proven to be the children or grandchildren of Christians who had not been in trouble with the Inquisition were permitted to emigrate to the Indies), and arranging for cargoes for his ships as far as Santo Domingo, it was September, 1563, before Ayllón, the younger, sailed for Española. By then it was known that the colonists Ribault left behind had fled from Port Royal and were in France. Thus there was no danger that Ayllón's colony would have to fight the French.

Ayllón's plan was to winter at Santo Domingo and then set out in the spring with two small ships, his colonists, and supplies. During the winter of 1563-1564, however, the expedition broke up amid demands by some of the would-be colonists for repayment of monies they had given to Ayllón for their passages. One story has it that Ayllón fled the island to escape their suits; another claims that he died of mortification at the failure of his venture. Whatever the truth, the expedition never got beyond Santo Domingo.

While Ayllón, the younger, had been preparing his expedition, the two Indians from the Chesapeake Bay were being returned to their home via Mexico—or at least that is what Philip II ordered. Clothed and provided with passages at royal expense, these men were given over to the care of Pedro Menéndez de Avilés, captain general of a convoy sailing to Mexico in the spring of 1562. Menéndez de Avilés was to send the Indians home by way of a dispatch boat from Mexico, along with news of his arrival and of the date that he expected to sail for Spain in the spring of 1563. By this time, one of the two Indians was known as Don Luis de Velasco, in honor of the viceroy of Mexico who had sponsored the Luna and Villafañe voyages.

The Indians duly arrived in Mexico but were so ill that their lives were despaired of. Fearing death, they asked to be baptized. In time they recovered, as a result of nursing by the Dominican friars at Mexico City; however, they missed the chance to return to their homeland with the dispatch boat. The viceroy of Mexico eventually agreed with the request of the Dominicans that these two converts be kept in Mexico until a suitable means could be found to return them to their native country. The Indians remained in Mexico for the next four years.

At the same time that Lucas Vázquez de Ayllón, the younger, was fitting for his voyage and the Indians were being sent home, Philip II gave to the governor of Cuba orders to scout out the French colony reported to be at 30 degrees north latitude and, if possible, to drive it from the coast. After some delay, Hernán Manrique de Rojas was sent in a small boat to carry out these orders. He failed to find the colony, which had departed almost a year before his voyage of 1564, but he did find one Frenchman living among the Indians, as well as the French fort and one of the stone pillars that Ribault had erected to mark the territories of the king of France. These discoveries made it clear that safeguarding the Spanish claim to the Point of Santa Elena and Port Royal Sound would require more vigorous actions than those taken by Villafañe in 1561.

Menéndez de Avilés, meanwhile, returned to Spain from Mexico, was arrested for smuggling, and fled to court after jumping bail when he was released to attend to a ship he owned. At court he pressed his case and offered himself as the leader of an expedition to settle in Florida. Philip was looking for such a leader, for by early 1565 he had learned that Ayllón, the younger, had failed to make good the king's claim to North America by occupying at least one point on the coast. Furthermore, Philip had information that the French were planning to dispatch a colony to replace the one Ribault had

11

In 1565 Pedro Menéndez de Avilés agreed to undertake a hasty voyage to the New World to defend Florida against the threat of settlement by the French. Arriving in the nick of time, he successfully repelled a French force and founded the Spanish fortifications of St. Augustine and Santa Elena. Menéndez subsequently led a number of Spanish expeditions to the area of Chesapeake Bay. Detail of engraving from Lowery, *The Spanish Settlements within the Present Limits of the United States: Florida, 1562-1574*, frontispiece.

established. Menéndez de Avilés, as was his custom, told the king what he wanted to hear. He offered the resources of his kinsmen as well as himself; expressed a great desire to search for his only son, who had been lost at sea in 1564 while on a voyage home from Mexico; and proposed all sorts of schemes for developing a prosperous colony in which Spaniards would work hard and Indians would be converted to Christianity by peaceful means. In the end, Menéndez in early March, 1565, signed a contract for the colonization of Florida.

Within days of signing the contract, Menéndez was called back to sign a new document. The king had just learned that the French had indeed established a colony in Florida and were preparing to reinforce it. As if to prove the worst suspicions of the Spanish, this news came from men captured in the Greater Antilles when they tried to overpower Spanish ships. A nest of heretical pirates had been established in Florida! The king offered to supply troops and a bonus if Menéndez de Avilés could get his expedition to sea within three months. If he did, it might get to Florida before the reinforcements under Ribault reached the peninsula.

Menéndez made the deadline. Although his fleet was scattered by a storm as it crossed the Atlantic, he pushed on with the few ships he could assemble at Puerto Rico. In late August, 1565, he landed at the site of St. Augustine. Ribault had arrived in Florida before him and threatened to disrupt the unloading of Menéndez's men and supplies. But another storm drove Ribault down the coast and wrecked his ships off Cape Canaveral, while giving Menéndez cover for a march against the French at Fort Caroline (near present-day Jacksonville, Florida). Following the Spanish victory there, he founded St. Augustine and later Santa Elena, on present-day Parris Island, South Carolina.

Important as these achievements were, Menéndez de Avilés had yet another goal. His letters indicate that he was greatly impressed by what he had heard from the two Indian guests during the voyage to Mexico in the spring of 1562 and wanted to travel to their country. Aware of what Villafañe had reported about the River of Santa Elena and the Jordan River, he proposed to go to the area from which these Indians had come, for it was said to be better and more densely populated land than the areas Villafañe had explored. Moreover, in gathering information to support his petition to the king in 1564, Menéndez had come across the idea that there was a way from near Bahia de Santa Maria across land to the arm of the Pacific Ocean that came near to the Atlantic at that point. These ideas were subsequently reinforced by the geographical information, including maps, he secured when he captured Fort Caroline.

The two Indians, he knew, came from that general area. As Christians and natives they would constitute a way of identifying a rich field for missions, provide an example for their brothers to imitate, and give Menéndez access to the passage to China and a backdoor route to the mines of northern Mexico, which he thought were not far south of the arm of the Pacific that bisected the continent. To pursue this imperial vision, Menéndez needed only to get the Indians from Mexico. At his request, Philip II ordered Don Luis de Velasco sent to Havana. Without any authority but their own, Don Luis's Dominican hosts decided to send two of their number to accompany him on whatever mission the adelantado might have in mind.

The party from Mexico arrived at St. Augustine in July, 1566. Suitably augmented with men from the Florida garrison, the friars, Don Luis de Velasco, and an escort left San Mateo (the Spanish name for Fort Caroline) on August 2. On August 14 they landed at about 37 degrees 30 minutes north latitude, probably at the entrance to Chincoteague Bay, Maryland. As they were sounding the entrance to the bay, a storm blew up and drove their ship out to sea. When they again made the coast on the twenty-fourth, they were at 36 degrees north latitude. Recent scholarship has concluded that they

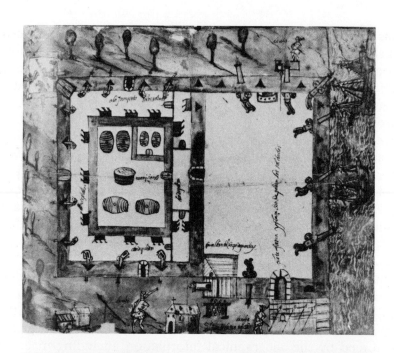

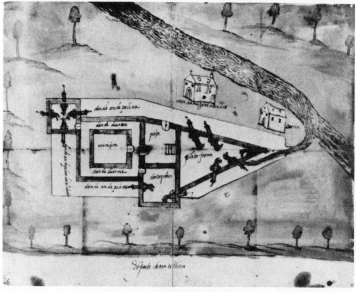

In 1565 a Spanish expedition under Pedro Menéndez de Avilés established a garrison at St. Augustine in Florida, thus founding Spain's first settlement on the east coast of North America. The drawing at top depicts the fortification at St. Augustine as it appeared in 1577. The drawing at bottom shows the Spanish fort at Santa Elena. Both drawings courtesy the Archivo General de Indias, Seville, Spain.

14

then entered Currituck Sound, North Carolina. No Indians were found either on the barrier islands or up the sound, nor did Don Luis recognize the land as his own, despite his earlier boasts that it stretched from 36 degrees to 39 degrees north latitude.

Setting sail again for the earlier landfall, the voyagers experienced adverse winds that delayed their arrival at that place until September 3. Once again as they came to anchor a strong land wind arose and drove the ship to sea, where a storm blew for three days. Seeing that the storm continued, and noting that the time limit for the voyage had been exceeded, the commander decided to sail for Spain. He had no desire to be caught on the American coast during hurricane season and had dispatches from Menéndez to deliver to the king. Over the protests of the Dominican friars, who wanted to return to Florida to await a new opportunity to go to Don Luis's land, he set the ship's course to the east. The vessel entered Cadiz harbor on October 23.

Menéndez did not give up his interest in the Chesapeake Bay area, but it was 1570 before he was again able to send an expedition there. Evidently he did not have as much confidence in the stories of the bay as a point of access to the eastern arm of the South Sea (Pacific Ocean) as his letters of 1564-1565 suggest. The sending of missionaries rather than soldiers and settlers seems a strange way to follow up on such a potentially profitable bit of knowledge. Perhaps Menéndez realized that this theory was wrong because of the information brought back by expeditions of Captain Juan Pardo into present-day western North Carolina and eastern Tennessee in 1566-1568. Pardo got a better idea of the geography of the interior of the continent than had anyone since Hernando de Soto's explorations in 1539-1542. Pardo's reports are silent on the subject of an arm of the Pacific north of the mountains he skirted and crossed. Given Menéndez's interest in the geography he had learned from his French captives and their papers, among other sources, Pardo surely would have commented had he heard anything from his Indian hosts about an arm of the sea.

Menéndez's expedition of 1570 landed a party of Jesuits and Don Luis on the western shore of the Chesapeake Bay, possibly on the York Peninsula. Contrary to expectations, Don Luis quickly reverted to his native ways and eventually organized a war party that killed all of the missionaries except for a servant boy, who was visiting an Indian village and was protected by its chief. This boy was eventually recovered by the Spanish, who became suspicious when supply ships sent out in 1571 were atacked by the Indians. Menéndez led the next

During the voyage of Pedro Menéndez de Avilés to the Chesapeake Bay in
1570, the Indian Don Luis de Velasco
organized a Powhatan Indian war
party that attacked and killed a
number of Jesuit missionaries who
sailed with Menéndez. The execution
of the Jesuits is depicted in this engraving entitled "The Killing of Father
Seguro and His Companions." Engraving from Mathias Tanner, *Societas Jesu
Usque ad Sanguinis et Vitae Profu-
sionem Militans* . . . (Prague: Typis
Universitatis Carolo-Ferdinandae,
1675), plate VII.

expedition to the bay, in 1572. After recovering the boy, he wreaked
such vengeance as he could on the Indians but did not attack their
villages. He never returned. Menéndez de Avilés's death in 1574
removed the one Spaniard of his generation who had both an interest
in the Atlantic seaboard north of Cape Hatteras and the means to
do something about exploring or even occupying a part of it.

In sum, Spanish voyages along the Outer Banks and up to and
beyond Chesapeake Bay were few in number prior to 1586 and
resulted in unfavorable reports. This negative image of the area and
its resources was partially overcome by the reports of Don Luis de
Velasco, the Indian from Chesapeake Bay, and by the French
cartographic tradition that began with Verrazzano's voyage of 1524.
The French tradition held that the Outer Banks were really a peninsula on whose western side lay the Pacific Ocean or, alternatively,
that an arm of the Pacific came to within a short distance of one of
the bays that lay at about 37 degrees north latitude, specifically Bahia
de Santa Maria. The possibility that Don Luis's homeland bordered
not only on Bahia de Santa Maria but also on the mountains across
which lay the Pacific led the Spanish under Menéndez de Avilés to
attempt to establish missions there in 1566 and again in 1570. The
failure of those attempts, because of unfavorable weather and In-

16

dian hostilities, diminished Spanish interest in Bahia de Santa Maria. Even so, this burst of activity associated with Chesapeake Bay focused Spanish interest on that area, with the result that the Spanish neglected the exploration of the coast between there and Santa Elena. That stretch of coast was dismissed as a long series of sand islands cut by a few rivers and tidal estuaries difficult to enter because of sandbars. It was, to quote again the cosmographer Alonso de Santa Cruz, a coast of desert islands, useless so far as the Spanish were concerned.

II. Spain, England, and the First News of the Roanoke Colony

The founding of an English colony on the Atlantic coast of North America in 1585 and the Spanish effort to locate and destroy it in the years that followed characterize the state into which Anglo-Spanish relations had fallen by the late 1580s. But they had not always been so. Nor had Spanish responses to foreign intrusion always taken the lackadaisical course they took in this case. In Spain's defense, it must be noted that events in 1585 and later years were without precedent in the history of the Spanish Empire in the Caribbean, a situation that figured significantly in the slow pace of the Spanish response.

From the signing of the Treaty of Medina del Campo in 1490 until the divorce of Henry VIII from Catherine of Aragon in 1533, English merchants enjoyed unmolested access to Spanish and, after 1503, Spanish-American markets. Their agents are known to have been in Spain's American possessions during the 1520s. So numerous were these English merchants in southern Spain that even before 1490 the dukes of Medina Sidonia, who owned the port town of San Lucar de Barameda, had granted them the right to create in that town their own court to judge disputes among themselves. By the early sixteenth century, many Englishmen appear to have married Spanish women and settled in Andalusia. Their trade primarily involved the exchange of English textiles and iron for Spanish wines and olive oil and the products of the New World that poured into Seville.

Following Henry's divorce and the creation of the Church of England, Spanish officials and merchants began to harass English merchants, especially transients who came to southern Spain with merchandise to sell but had no fixed residence in the peninsula. The harassment centered on the question of who was head of the church in England. The Spanish did not recognize Henry, or his Protestant successors, as head of the church. Englishmen, however, were required to recognize Henry as head of the church and even, after 1534, to swear an oath to that effect. With the passage of time and the increasingly Protestant tenor of the Church of England's theological positions and ritual, the Spanish gradually enlarged the religious subject matter about which to question Englishmen. Any Englishman who responded that the pope was not head of the church in England, or answered some theological question in a way that sounded Protestant to the sometimes ill-informed Spanish clergy of Andalusia, or was found to possess an English translation of the Bible or Protestant religious literature, might quickly find himself denounced to the Inquisition.

Arrest by the Inquisition on suspicion of heresy meant not only jail and a trial in which the accused could not confront his accusers or even learn their identities, but also the confiscation of all property in the arrested person's possession, whether his own or that of a second party. Thus, merchants in England could lose their goods because of the religious views of their agents who visited Spain, or even because of a drunken slip of the tongue in the presence of hostile Spaniards bent on driving a commercial rival from their market.

Modern studies have demonstrated that relatively few Englishmen were actually arrested by the Inquisition in southern Spain, but the reputation of the Spanish for religious intolerance made it seem that any Englishman who ventured to Andalusia was likely to forfeit his property and perhaps his life. Moreover, that reputation grew so that in 1569-1574 Spain and England came close to breaking diplomatic relations. This crisis resulted from Philip II's expulsion of the English ambassador for attempting to practice his religion openly in Madrid and from Elizabeth I's retaliation by "protecting" monies being shipped to the duke of Alba's army in the Netherlands by confiscating them. One of the English demands was that goods of an absent principal not be subject to confiscation if that principal's agent in Spain got into trouble with the Inquisition. Over objections from within his government, Philip II acceded to this demand. Nonetheless, it was clear that trade between England and southern Spain was difficult at best and subject to possible interruption should diplomatic relations deteriorate further.

As early as 1563 John Hawkins had attempted to find a way around this religious obstacle to continued trade with Spain by sailing directly to the Caribbean and engaging in peaceful trade that included payment of all taxes and fees, and he even sent a portion of his return cargo to Seville. But the Spanish rejected all such efforts to operate outside the system of permits and inspections set forth in Spanish law. Hawkins's later voyages (in 1565 and 1568) met increasing resistance from Spaniards resident in the Caribbean. In Europe, diplomatic relations deteriorated because of differing national interests in the Low Countries and over religion. As noted, events of 1569-1574 nearly led to a break in all relations between Spain and England.

Richard Hakluyt, the younger, drew an obvious conclusion: the English should seek sources of supplies that the Spanish could not interrupt. In his *Discourse of Western Planting* (1585) Hakluyt advanced the idea that a colony in the middle latitudes of North America could supply England with olive oil, wine, silk, and access to the tropical goods normally acquired from southern Spain or by raiding Spanish shipping in Caribbean or European waters. This assertion suggests that Hakluyt was familiar with the geographic theory that similar climates and resources existed at the same latitudes north and south of the equator, as well as with the writings of Peter Martyr. Martyr, it will be recalled, had reported Lucas Vázquez de Ayllón's tale of the new Andalusia in North America. Hakluyt's *Discourse* was written in support of the Ralegh-Gilbert voyages, in particular those Walter Ralegh was planning to the middle latitudes of North America.

By 1583 Walter Ralegh had determined to seek a suitable site for a colony south of the area that Sir Humphrey Gilbert had explored in the 1570s in his fruitless search for a Northwest Passage to the Orient. Ralegh's options were limited by the presence of the Spanish at St. Augustine and at Santa Elena and by their relative control over the Indians along the coast between. On the other hand, Ralegh seems already to have come in contact with the Portuguese pilot Simão Fernandes, or Simon Ferdinando, as he was known in English. According to his subsequent boasts to some Spanish captives held for several years by Sir Richard Grenville, Fernandes convinced Ralegh and his associates that he, Fernandes, knew of a port or ports at the correct latitude (that is, the same latitude as Andalusia) and that that was the place for the colony. In the spring of 1584 Ralegh gave Fernandes the opportunity to make good his boast by sending him as a pilot with Philip Amadas and Arthur Barlowe on a reconnaissance along the Florida coast.

Keeping track of the departures of other Europeans—the Spanish commonly called them corsairs—from Europe for the Caribbean was an established aspect of Spain's policy for the defense of its American possessions. When, in addition, spies or diplomats were able to find out the plans of the interlopers, that information was forwarded as part of a warning to the king's officials in the principal ports of the Caribbean. These officials were thus able to prepare local defenses. Should a major fleet be known to sail, especially with intent to seize a port or ports in the Caribbean, the government in Spain could mobilize troops and ships to counter such a move. The expense of large fixed garrisons was thus avoided, without too much danger that any part of the empire would fall to an enemy's fleet. The system had worked well against the Ribault voyages of 1562-1563 and 1564-1565, especially the latter. After 1559 peace with France and England provided the Spanish with full diplomatic opportunities to monitor the voyages of the two nations.

The bases of this system of intelligence gathering were secret pensions paid to highly placed members of both governments willing to share information and agents hired to go to seaports to mix with seamen and listen to their talk. But much depended upon the zeal, intelligence, and character of the resident ambassador. In all of those respects Philip II was well served until the 1580s, when Bernardino de Mendoza let his religious beliefs and hatred of the Protestant English get between his master's interests and the English. Exasperated by Mendoza's involvement in plots centering on Mary, Queen of Scots, and by his hectoring tone in interviews and written communications, Elizabeth's government expelled him from England in January, 1584. When he departed, he left behind in London an agent funded and instructed to keep him informed of developments, especially those involving English voyages to the New World.

In the spring of 1584 Mendoza's agent reported that a number of ships were being prepared for voyages to the Indies. By early April, however, a lack of funds had caused most of the preparations to cease. Only Ralegh's "little vessel" and four belonging to Christopher Carleill, the stepson of secretary of state Sir Francis Walsingham, were still fitting. The "little vessel" was the ship in which Amadas and Barlowe and Simon Fernandes sailed to Florida that spring. The agent also believed that William Hawkins, brother of John Hawkins, was again fitting out a fleet, as he had done in 1583 when his passage through the Antilles with seven ships and their crews, as well as women passengers, caused the governor of Puerto Rico to suspect that he was seeking a place to establish a settlement.

Mendoza, meanwhile, had established himself in Paris as Philip's ambassador to France. In late February, 1585, with his information network in England still intact, he reported that in January Elizabeth had knighted Walter Ralegh and promised to pay the cost of the voyage Ralegh was planning, should he be unable to sail. This curious arrangement probably indicates that Elizabeth anticipated that the Marques de Santa Cruz might attack England in the summer of 1585. Santa Cruz was, in fact, preparing a fleet at Lisbon for that very purpose. Philip had decided to bring an end to English support of his Dutch rebels (as he called them) and of Don Antonio, prior of Crato and pretender to the Portuguese throne, which Philip had seized in 1580. The timing of the attack on England was dependent, however, on completion of arrangements for Scottish or even French Catholic support for Mary, Queen of Scots, Elizabeth's prisoner and the figurehead around whom Catholic Englishmen were expected to rally once the Spanish-Scottish invasion forces were in England. To meet the naval portion of this threat, Elizabeth would have diverted Ralegh's ships to the defense of the realm. She had a similar arrangement with Sir Francis Drake, who was preparing a fleet for action against the Spanish.

Ralegh's fleet consisted of one of the queen's own ships—the *Tiger*, of 180 tons, with ten guns on the sides and two at the bow—along with two Dutch flyboats of 120 tons burden each (for supplies) and two barks or pinnaces of 40 tons each. This fleet was to be ready to sail from London at the beginning of March. Its destination was said to be Norembega, the Indian town on the Penobscot River (in present-day Maine) that had become a feature on maps of the North American coast. The town was just south of the cod fishing banks off Newfoundland. It is known that Ralegh intended to attack the Spanish and Portuguese fishing fleets off Newfoundland and did so in 1585. The identification of Norembega as the destination of his fleet hinted at his plans to create a colony in North America and to attack the fisheries. Nevertheless, such identification was misleading because Amadas and Barlowe had returned in 1584 with news of the sounds behind the Outer Banks, the expedition's eventual destination.

In the same letter in which he provided the information just noted, Mendoza reported that Sir Francis Drake was preparing twenty-four ships to carry 2,000 men to attack Spanish convoys and Nombre de Dios, the Caribbean port through which flowed the trade across the

Isthmus of Panama. This report was closer to the truth, if still short of the grand design Drake implemented in the first six months of 1586.

In letters dated March 15 and April 18, Mendoza was able to report not only the departure of Ralegh's ships from London for a voyage to Portsmouth but also that the fleet that assembled there consisted of five ships and as many as eight pinnaces, rather an exaggeration. English sources reveal that only seven ships sailed on April 19, 1585.

By the end of April Mendoza was reporting that the ships had sailed, while from Lisbon the Marques de Santa Cruz reported that an Englishman who had left England on April 12 said that one Richard Granvelle (Grenville), a "principal man of England," had assembled altogether thirty ships, mostly small, for a voyage to a place called "Naranvel," located between Florida and Newfoundland. This fleet was carrying men and equipment for settling. It was believed in Lisbon that it would have sailed by the end of April. Santa Cruz, like Mendoza, also reported on Francis Drake's preparations, but without any information as to Drake's purpose.

Mendoza next supplied information to Philip in a letter dated June 1. Reports from England had it that a storm had scattered Grenville's fleet (which was true) and that the ships had put back into England (which was not true). Santa Cruz's report of June 11 clarified the strength of the expedition as seven small ships but added nothing concerning its destination or fate. This information augmented what was known in Madrid but was irrelevant by the time it was received. Grenville had already reached the Caribbean, where local observers gained a clear picture of his strength and intentions.

In London, Mendoza's agent was arrested in mid-May. Obtaining accurate information from the island proved to be increasingly difficult during the next few years as Spain and England drifted rapidly into a war that did not formally end until 1603.

Grenville's fleet was scattered by a storm while still in European waters. A rendezvous off the south coast of Puerto Rico had been arranged for just such an eventuality. Accordingly, Grenville proceeded on his way aboard the *Tiger*, arriving at a place called Las Boquillas, Puerto Rico, on May 20. While some of his crewmen dug a ditch around the camp, creating a low rampart, others built a forge and began to construct two pinnaces. The Spanish quickly learned of this presence and sent a force of forty men from San German to watch the camp. Under a flag of truce the Spanish force made contact with Grenville's men, who told them that they had come to trade and were bound for Mexico. But a few days later, on the twenty-eighth, Grenville was joined by another of his larger ships, the *Elizabeth,* which arrived with two prizes taken off Mona Island, just to the west. One carried a shipment of cloth that had been sent from Santo Domingo to San Juan. The other was engaged in local trade and appears not to have held cargo of any value.

As the Spanish watched and additional troops were ordered to march from San Juan to the English camp, the pinnaces were completed and launched. Finally the English erected a post on which they had carved the message: "On May 11 we reached this place in the Tiger and on the 19th the Elizabeth came up and we are about to leave on the 23rd in good health, glory be to God, 1585." That done, Grenville and his fleet sailed for San German. Arriving there on June 1, they offered to ransom their prizes (but not the captured cloth) for hogs, young cattle, horses, and other supplies. Under orders from the governor of Puerto Rico, Diego Menéndez de Valdés, this trade was refused. Undaunted, the English set sail for the northern coast of Española, where they could expect a friendlier reception.

The Spanish took the carved post to San Juan and forwarded to Havana a careful copy of its message, together with a letter that Menéndez de Valdés wrote on June 7 to his relative, Pedro Menéndez Marqués, the governor of Florida, who was in Havana preparing to sail to Spain on a voyage he had been seeking permission to make since 1581. To Menéndez de Valdés, the English camp was a prime example of how easily non-Spaniards could establish themselves on Puerto Rico because of its weak economy and scant population, deficiencies that had their origin in the lack of slave labor for sugar and other plantations. Menéndez de Valdés asked Menéndez Marqués to use this example in arguing before the Council of the Indies, an administrative, legislative, and judicial body empowered to develop and control large Spanish overseas possessions, for a number of benefits for the island of Puerto Rico and its governor— benefits the latter had been seeking without result up to that time. In a postscript, Menéndez de Valdés noted the effort of the English to obtain livestock at San German and concluded from this that they intended to make a settlement somewhere.

This letter reached Havana on June 19. Four days later, as officials at Havana were preparing to dispatch this information to the king, a ship entered that port from Bayaha, Española, with news that the English had been seen at Puerto Plata and La Isabela, Española, with five large ships. There they had repeated their demands for livestock, with some success. Fearing that the English would next arrive at Bayaha, the ship's master had fled that place to avoid capture. He also reported that aboard one of the ships was a man of importance who was served on silver plate and was thought by some persons to be Don Antonio, Philip's only rival for the Portuguese throne.

In reporting this news to Spain, officials in Havana concluded that this was the English fleet about which they had been warned. They accepted the idea that the English intended to settle somewhere in Florida or on a long island that lay in the Bahama Channel. In view of these possibilities, they asked that the king send his West Indies fleet to prevent such an eventuality. They also reported that French raiders were off Cape San Antonio. In short, the information concerning Grenville's voyage was treated as important, but not exceptionally so. Had Menéndez de Valdés's letter and the ship from Bayaha reached Havana a few days after they did, in all likelihood the news would not have been reported for months—until there was a news boat at hand to carry letters.

Pedro Menéndez Marqués, on the other hand, thought the possible colonizing efforts of the English serious enough to stop in St. Augustine on his way to Spain, in case the English intended to try to seize it or Santa Elena, both of which were weakly defended. When he arrived in St. Augustine on July 20, he found that the English had not disturbed it. However, Gutierre de Miranda, the man he had left in charge, had caused trouble by imposing rationing and setting the soldiers to work on a ditch and terreplein next to the fort, which was little more than a two-story board-covered warehouse with an artillery platform on the bay side. At the petition of almost everyone in town, Menéndez Marqués decided to remain in St. Augustine and in command until he could determine what the English were up to.

The news of the English and other corsairs reached La Terceira Island in the Azores about mid-July. As a merchant there understood it, a contingent of eighteen English ships and eight pinnaces was active in the Antilles and intended to settle an island "called Trinidad and Dominica," where it had left six ships. Apparently this was one version of their story that the English were telling Spaniards, for it was repeated by a man who had been captured while aboard one of the ships taken off Mona Island. It was, of course, a red herring so far as Grenville was concerned.

The reports of Grenville's passage through the Greater Antilles and his acquisition of livestock reached Seville on August 7. There appears to have been no immediate reaction to it. Such reports had come in before without having any substance: Menéndez de Valdés had reported colonizing expeditions in earlier years. His motives in doing so again were apparent in his letter of June 7 to Menéndez Marqués. Furthermore, the Council of the Indies was even then debating how many reinforcements and what sorts of supplies to send to Florida in response to requests by Pedro Menéndez Marqués in 1584.

More important, however, was the question of what Drake would do with the more than two dozen ships and 2,000 men he was reported to be preparing. His objectives were not known and could not be discovered because the English closed their country to foreign travelers and restricted the activities of those Englishmen who might have been willing to spy for Bernardino de Mendoza. A vague threat of an English colony somewhere in the vastness of North America south of the cod fisheries required inquiries, and one was sent in September by the president of the House of Trade to the warden of the fort at Havana; but until the warden or some other official could report specific details, more important matters occupied the king's agents and advisers in Spain.

The next reliable news available in Spain was contained in the deposition of Enrique Lopez, who had been captured by the English while aboard Alonso Corniele's ship as it sailed from Santo Domingo to Seville and was released at Flores in the Azores. Corniele's crew had mistaken Grenville's *Tiger* for a ship that had sailed at the same time. Lopez reported Grenville's name, described his ship, identified Simon Fernandes as his pilot, and gave a brief outline of his voyage in the Antilles and of the fact that he had left 300 men in a fort in Florida (exact location unknown). Grenville, according to Lopez, had sent a frigate to England to have supplies readied for an immediate return to his colony. Lopez failed to report that among the Spanish seamen Grenville did not free at Flores was Pedro Diaz, a pilot who, when he eventually escaped, provided a very detailed account of the Roanoke colonies up to 1588. Lopez dictated his deposition at Fayal in mid-November, 1585. It would have been available in Madrid by December 24, when the possibility of an English occupation of one of the Spanish towns in Florida was first mentioned in a document sent from the Council of the Indies to Philip II.

Keeping track of the activities and whereabouts of English explorers bound for the Caribbean was an established aspect of Spain's policy for the defense of its American possessions. Sir Richard Grenville attracted the attention of the Spanish in 1585 when he led a flotilla of English vessels on an expedition to the New World. Engraving of Grenville from Alexander Brown (ed.), *The Genesis of the United States* (Boston and New York: Houghton, Mifflin and Company, 2 volumes, 1890), I, facing p. 450.

In the Caribbean additional information concerning Grenville's activities was being gathered, but it did not arrive in Spain until January or even February, 1586, by which time several important events overshadowed it. It was reported that Indians in Florida had seen ships presumed to be Grenville's sail northward off the coast. From Santo Domingo the new crown attorney reported in more detail about the visit of the fleet in June, 1585, to Puerto Plata, near which the warden of the town's fort had been entertained by Grenville. From that interview it had been learned that the English were going to settle on the Florida coast "up towards the cod fisheries" and that they carried thirty pieces of artillery, 500 men and women, many plants from the Antilles, and livestock. This news confirmed what Bernardino de Mendoza had previously reported about English intentions and demonstrated that the English had done what they had planned to do. But where they were on the coast of Florida was still unknown.

This very uncertainty was cited by the Council of the Indies when it wrote to Philip II on December 24, again urging approval of Pedro Menéndez Marqués's request of 1584 for various munitions and for fifty soldiers to replace others who were disabled, dead, or had left Florida. The council wanted to send the men in a ship that Captain Juan de Posada, brother-in-law of Menéndez Marqués, was taking to Florida. Declaring that it was assumed that the English had gone to Florida to settle and that the lack of any information from there indicated an unfavorable development, the council urged this course rather than the slower one of sending the soldiers with a convoy scheduled to sail in the spring of 1586. The king approved the plan because of news that Drake was on his way to the Caribbean. As finally arranged, Posada sailed with the fleet in May, 1586, as far as Dominica, whence he sailed to St. Augustine. He arrived on July 19, just after Drake had left the burned, looted ruins of the town to move northward in search of Santa Elena and Roanoke.

Drake's attack on the Caribbean, beginning in January, 1586, signaled the opening of an Anglo-Spanish naval war that had been brewing for a generation. War became almost certain once Philip II decided to raise a fleet at Lisbon for an attack upon England, ostensibly to rescue Mary, Queen of Scots, and reestablish the Catholic religion, but in fact to try to force the English to stop aiding the Dutch and to cease attacking Spanish shipping in the Atlantic.

Of far greater concern to the Spanish was the English adventurer Sir Francis Drake, whose raid on Spanish outposts in the Caribbean in 1586 opened a new chapter in the history of Spain's defense of its Caribbean empire and diverted Spanish attention from locating the English settlement purported to have been established somewhere on the coast of Florida. Engraving of Drake from Brown, *The Genesis of the United States*, I, facing p. 350.

Drake's raid also opened a new chapter in the history of Spain's defense of its Caribbean empire. Drake had a force of more than 1,000 men, approximately ten times the size of a typical large raiding party used prior to his attack and two to five times larger than the militias of even the major Spanish port towns in the Caribbean. Given these odds, the scarcity of weapons and munitions for the militiamen, and the virtual absence of fortifications and walls around the cities, it is not surprising that Drake easily took Santo Domingo and Cartagena (Colombia). Had he wanted to, he might have taken Havana and the entire island of Cuba, in spite of the reinforcements it had received from Mexico. St. Augustine fell with little more than token resistance from a fort hastily erected at a point where its artillery could block the English entrance into the bay. In short, Drake demonstrated that substantial new defenses were needed if the English, or the Dutch or the French, were to be prevented from seizing one or more of the ports through which flowed the silver that helped make Philip II the most powerful monarch in Europe.

Meeting this urgent need meant that the king and his Council of the Indies had little time to worry about an English colony somewhere on the coast of Florida, once it became clear that the English had seized neither St. Augustine nor Santa Elena. For officials in the Caribbean, including those in Florida who had the responsibility of searching for the English settlement, interest in the colony was partially a matter of complying with royal orders to search for it and partially a function of reports of 1586 and 1589-1590 that Drake planned to use it as a base from which to raid the Caribbean again. The initial reports of the English colony were overshadowed by larger events, events that gave the Spanish reasons not to press the search for Roanoke with the same sort of vigor they had displayed in searching for Jean Ribault's colony of 1562. Without a vigorous search, information about the English colony's location and history accumulated slowly in St. Augustine, Havana, and Madrid.

III. The Search for the English Colony Begins, 1586-1587

Sir Francis Drake's passage through the Caribbean Sea left in its wake not only the smoking ruins of Santo Domingo, Cartagena, and St. Augustine but also men who had been held captive for brief periods. The testimony of these men, gathered at Havana and St. Augustine, and what was known of Drake's activities at Santo Domingo and Cartagena provided the Spanish with additional evidence that the English had a colony on the North American coast "towards the cod fisheries." Receipt of this news in Spain in the autumn of 1586 led to consideration of the immediate relief of Florida's distress and also of the future of the colony and how it could be made more viable without great cost to the king's treasury. The colony's future appeared to be tied to the location, purpose, and survivability of the English settlement. From these considerations came the first orders to search for the English colony. A search was to be conducted with an eye toward moving the Spanish colony to a more favorable location, possibly the one occupied by the English.

On September 3, 1586, Pedro Bernal Cremeño brought his small ship into port at Seville. He had come from Havana with letters from officials there telling the crown what had happened during the two months prior to his departure on July 4. These documents reported the good news that Drake had sailed by Havana. They also reported that Drake had attacked St. Augustine in early June, occupied it after a pro forma defense by its garrison, looted it, and burned it before sailing northward in search of the other Spanish town, Santa Elena. Reports from St. Augustine forwarded from Havana indicated that Drake's objective in Florida was Santa Elena. He had attacked St. Augustine only because the Portuguese pilot he carried for the Florida coast had pointed out that he was about to bypass it. Everyone at Havana felt certain that Santa Elena would have fallen to Drake, but they had no news of this when they closed their letters on July 4.

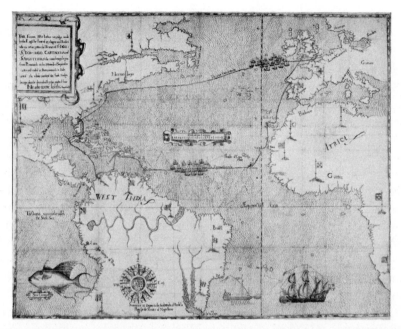

Sir Francis Drake's raids on Spanish shipping and fortifications in the Caribbean in 1586 heightened Spanish anxiety concerning the possibility that England might utilize a settlement in North America as a base for additional attacks. As a result, Pedro Menéndez Marqués, Spanish governor of Florida, ordered Vicente González, a veteran pilot of the Florida coast, to search for the feared English colony. This map (1589) traces the route of Drake's fleet. Map reproduced courtesy the British Library Board.

Furthermore, a man who had been a prisoner in Drake's fleet but fled at Cape San Antonio (in western Cuba) reported that Drake was going to the cod fisheries to find out if the Spanish fleet had sailed to attack England. If it had, and had successfully invaded, Drake apparently planned to take his fleet to North Africa. If the Spanish had not attacked England, it was believed that he would winter at Santa Elena or at the English colony and return to the Caribbean the following spring to conduct yet more raids, including one at Havana. The fact that Drake had taken several hundred black and Indian slaves from the Caribbean colonies and had stripped St. Augustine of everything that would be useful for a settlement strengthened the belief at Havana that he intended to reinforce the English colony, or perhaps to establish his own, and use it as a springboard for raids during 1587. Don Antonio, the pretender to the Portuguese throne, was supposed to join Drake in 1587, apparently in the hope of seizing territory on which to reestablish his claim to the throne.

31

As to the question of where the English colony was located, all but one of the authorities in Havana reported only "towards the cod fisheries." The exception was Alonso Suarez, a prominent citizen of Toledo. In a letter dated June 27 he linked the Grenville voyage of 1585, which collected livestock and plants in the Antilles, to Drake's supposed plan to winter at the English colony, declaring that the earlier voyage was made by Drake's order. He then asserted that the colony was at Bahia de Santa Maria (Chesapeake Bay). Suarez had been there in 1572 with Pedro Menéndez de Avilés, and he described the bay as having "a good climate, thickly populated country, with great plantings and stores of maize on the cob in great closed houses, vast meadows, the aborigines [illegible] and without arms, wild fruits like those of our Spain."[2] Suarez claimed that this description came from two men who escaped from Drake at Cape San Antonio, but the recorded depositions of the two men fail to mention Bahia de Santa Maria. Suarez apparently guessed that the English would select the best bay on the South Atlantic coast.

A far less likely explanation for Suarez's belief that the English were established at Bahia de Santa Maria is that he somehow had knowledge of information the Spanish administrator of Jamaica dispatched to King Philip II on the same date, June 27. The administrator's letter reported that in December, 1585, he had picked up on the northwestern coast of Jamaica two Englishmen, apparently the sole survivors among more than twenty who had been set ashore by the master of the ship in which they had come from England. This was one of Grenville's ships, and one of the men was Edward, who claimed to be a gentleman, an accountant, and second-in-command in the Grenville fleet. In a deposition taken on December 7, 1585, Edward told that a Portuguese pilot named Fernando (Simon Fernandes) had visited a headland on the Florida coast in 1577. Shown a map, Edward pointed the headland out. On the Spanish map it was situated at 38.5 degrees north latitude, but Edward said that it was shown at 36 degrees north on the English charts.

There was a bay with a good anchorage that led to certain islands and to a source of fresh water 4 leagues from the sea. This bay was alleged to be the best on the Atlantic coast and to have offered a way to the "other sea" (the Pacific Ocean). Gold, silver, and hides had been obtained from friendly Indians there, and two of the natives had been taken to England, with two Englishmen left as hostages in their place. The 1585 voyage was returning to that spot with the

Indians to build two forts, which would eventually house 1,000 people. Edward's ship had sailed in the company of five others but had become separated from the rest during a storm 100 leagues out from England. It had arrived in the Caribbean in desperate need of food and water and had made for Jamaica. There the ship's master put Edward and about twenty others ashore and abandoned them. Nine of these men died from hunger, and the rest went into the interior of the island in search of food and were thought to be dead.

The information that Edward gave in Jamaica in December, 1585, was the most accurate description of the location of the English colony that the Spanish would obtain for nearly three years. The entrance through the Outer Banks to Roanoke was situated at almost precisely 36 degrees north latitude, and Roanoke is one of several islands in the sounds. Fresh water could be found 12 or so nautical miles up Albemarle Sound. On the other hand, the notion that the sounds provided access to the "other sea" may have been Edward's understanding of French cartography based on Verrazzano rather than what the Indians had told Philip Amadas and Arthur Barlowe. Or, this idea could have arisen from a statement by the Indians that Chesapeake Bay could be reached from the sounds.

Accurate as Edward's deposition was as to the site Grenville had in fact occupied, it seems not to have been credited in Spain or in the Caribbean save, possibly, by Suarez de Toledo, who put his own interpretation on it. Suarez based this interpretation on Spanish maps that showed a bay with islands at about 38 degree north, the latitude of Bahia de Santa Maria or Jacán, the Spanish name for the area around the bay. It is curious that the Spanish did not appreciate the importance of this information from Jamaica. In 1565, depositions taken on Jamaica from deserters from Fort Caroline had provided information that led to Menéndez de Avilés's expedition of that year. Yet, the 1585 report appears to have been ignored. Several factors may account for this. Edward spoke of where Fernandes had been in 1577 rather than where Grenville had gone. There was a difference in latitude between the place he pointed out on the Spanish map and where he said the English planned to go. Not least important, the administrator of Jamaica admitted at the very end of his covering letter that communication with Edward was difficult because they had no common language. And it is possible that Edward did not live to reach Seville, where competent translators would have been found. Without the man to give testimony in person, his information probably seemed less valuable than it actually was. The Spanish thus missed an opportunity to discover the Roanoke colony in 1587.

Alonso Suarez de Toledo's correspondence is of interest for a reason other than what he had to say about the location of the English colony. In a letter of July 3 Suarez suggested that Florida be abandoned:

To maintain Florida is merely to incur expenses because it is and has been entirely unprofitable nor can it sustain its own population. Everything must be brought from outside. If, although Your Majesty possesses Santo Domingo, Puerto Rico, Cuba, Yucatan, and New Spain [Mexico], the garrison of Florida has nevertheless suffered actual hunger, what would happen to foreigners there who must bring their subsistence from a great distance to an inhospitable coast? The land itself would wage war upon them. To say that they can maintain a base there from which to damage the convoys is idle talk because from Cape Canaveral, which is the end of the Bahama Channel, to St. Augustine is a bay of 50 leagues and dangerous coast. Let Your Majesty improve this harbor [Havana] instead, and fortify it, and send the galleons and the fleet on this course. That is what is needed, and plain speaking.[3]

Three days earlier Suarez had learned of the destruction of St. Augustine by Drake. Emergency relief was on the way, but the time was right for the king to consider whether to continue pouring money into the sands of Florida, where both of the towns built at great cost to the treasury had been destroyed, so far as Suarez knew.

From St. Augustine, Pedro Menéndez Marqués wrote to the king on July 17 reporting that Drake had passed by Santa Elena at night. Entering the port of Oristan (probably Saint Helena Sound), he had taken on wood and water and a mast for one of his ships. Menéndez Marqués expressed his opinion that Drake or others would return to take Florida because they had found it so fruitful and well cultivated. St. Augustine was particularly suited to their piratical purposes because it lay along the route of all shipping departing the Caribbean. Menéndez Marqués thus stated the case for retaining St. Augustine, a case that would be made many times during the ensuing twenty years because opinions of men like Suarez de Toledo caused the Council of the Indies periodically to consider the relocation of all the Florida settlements.

The carrier of Menéndez Marqués's letter of July 17 was Vicente González, a veteran pilot of the Florida coast. He reached Seville in early September. From there he and the letters from Florida and

Havana went on to Madrid. Letters from other parts of the Caribbean were forwarded at the same time.

The letters were received in Madrid on September 9. The Council of the Indies met all that day to consider what advice it should give Philip II. On the tenth the council wrote to the king suggesting that artillery and munitions be sent to the Caribbean as requested by officials there, including Menéndez Marqués in Florida. Commenting on the suggestion by Menéndez Marqués that the two garrisons in Florida be combined into one, at St. Augustine, the council noted that for some time (from about 1580, if not earlier) it had advocated replacement of the Florida garrisons with a single small fort at the head of the Florida Keys (approximately where Miami is located at present) and patrols along the coast to the north by galleys based in Havana. These defenses would help sailors in distress and enable the coast to be watched at a cost less than that required to maintain the garrisons—even if a third galley had to be added to the two being prepared for service at Havana. Continued efforts to settle the province should be made by private contractors rather than the king. Finally, the council discussed the need for a new fleet of galleons to patrol the Caribbean. In reply to the suggestion concerning the relocation of the Florida garrisons, the king asked that he be advised whether the forts were at ports that should be denied to an enemy.

The council's memorandum to the king demonstrates that it had accepted the idea of modifying the pattern of Spanish occupation in Florida in order to save money. The funds thus saved would be used to provide galleys for Havana, which would constitute a local defense for that key port and the seas around it—a plan that the governor, Gabriel de Luxan, had advocated since the idea of galleys as local patrol boats had been proposed in the 1570s. As recently as June 5, 1585, the governor had renewed his call of 1582 for galleys to replace all of the Florida forts.

The idea of retaining a coast guard station at the head of the Florida Keys had been advocated as early as 1580 by treasury officials in Florida, who were at odds with Pedro Menéndez Marqués. But their advocacy was probably a reflection of ideas they knew were already held by members of the Council of the Indies. Since perhaps 1580, no one except the lieutenant governor of Santa Elena, Gutierre de Miranda, had spoken in favor of more than one Florida settlement.

The location and the size of the proposed garrison were the only issues. Other than at St. Augustine and the head of the Keys, a few men in Florida had advocated placing the settlement north of Santa Elena at a port that would provide access to the backcountry, where rumor had it that there were mines and better soils. Concern about the English colony and what it might portend for Spanish control of the North American coast was not a factor in these deliberations, perhaps because the council believed that the coast was such a difficult place to settle that no foreign colony would long survive there.

In reply to the request by Philip II for additional information, the question of the fate of Florida was referred to the Junta de Puerto Rico on September 19. The junta had been established in 1580 as a temporary committee to consider the defenses of Puerto Rico, but it had become a permanent advisory body that concerned itself with defenses throughout the Caribbean. On September 29 it heard testimony from Vicente González, who discussed the fact that the exit from the Bahama Channel was located at the latitude of Cape Canaveral, from which point it was 35 leagues to St. Augustine. Between St. Augustine and Santa Elena were fourteen ports, many of them better harbors than either of those two. For defense of the Bahama Channel, González recommended consolidation of the garrison at St. Augustine, with the replacement of fifty men in the existing garrisons, which numbered 300 (290, according to the detailed figures he gave). That number would be adequate to defend the port against a new attack by Drake. But for settlement of a large number of men, González recommended the "rich land" that he described in another memorandum—a land to which he had been and which could be reached by a direct voyage from Spain without having to go via the Antilles, as was the case with St. Augustine.

The other memorandum of which González spoke has heretofore been ascribed to a date after 1600 and is believed to be his inaccurate recollection of the voyage he made in 1588 in search of the English. In fact, as the documents here reviewed make clear, the memorandum dates from September, 1586, and refers to a voyage he made to Cayagua—the Indian name for present Charleston harbor—in 1582. On that occasion González was searching for a French fort reported to have been built at or near Cayagua. He claimed that while coasting north he entered a port whose mouth was 2 leagues wide and extended 30 leagues into the land, with a maximum width of 6 leagues. This bay reached the foot of a mountain range, where there was a "principal chief" who dominated many other Indians. This chief had gold that he said came from mountains three days' journey away. He also had many pearls, although they were purple because the shellfish that contained them had been opened by being thrown into a fire.

González said that behind the mountain range at the end of the bay lay New Mexico, a mere five days' journey away. There were houses of four and five stories, many small cows (bison?), and much silver. Southwest of the bay were mountains with silver mines and diamond mines that had been visited by soldiers still in Florida. Moreover, around the bay were many plantations of maize, beans, and other foods.

As to the location of the English settlement, González claimed that the Indians had told him that it was situated on a river north of the place he had visited. He expressed the belief that this was the river "further on" that the Indians said led to the South Sea (Pacific Ocean). This port could be reached by a direct voyage from Spain.

As to the question of the consolidation of the garrisons in Florida, González said that they should be concentrated at St. Augustine but that some of the men should be sent to explore this bay and its surroundings. He felt certain that many men in Florida would be eager to go because of their belief in the richness of the area, which some had seen with their own eyes.

This was a cleverly drawn memorandum that combined the fact of González's voyage to Cayagua with geographic descriptions derived from his 1572 voyage to Chesapeake Bay and ideas he probably had picked up from Menéndez de Avilés concerning the ease of the portage from Chesapeake Bay to an arm of the South Sea. For his description of New Mexico he appropriated either knowledge gained from the tales of the explorer Alvar Núñez Cabeza de Vaca or the common report of what Francisco Vasquez de Coronado had found on his expedition northward from Mexico. González's tales of the silver and diamond mines inland from Cayagua were based on the journeys of Juan Pardo. Anyone knowledgeable about gems would have realized that the purple diamonds González described were merely purple quartz crystals. But González made the point that there was a rich interior area best reached from this unnamed port that lay north of Santa Elena. Equally important, the port would provide access to the English settlement. Finding wealth and the enemy's colony were objectives bound to interest the Spanish king or his advisers.

The undated memorandum from Vicente González that has confused historians for many years is pictured above and on the opposite page. The memorandum in fact dates from 1586 and reports on a voyage González made to present-day South Carolina in 1582. Thus, while the memorandum did not describe González's 1588 search for Sir Walter Ralegh's English colonies, as previously believed, it did influence directly Spain's decision to seek out English "corsairs" on the North American coast. Original memorandum held by the Archivo General de Indias; photograph supplied by the author.

Muchas minas de Plata y ay minas de cristal, Ay otra si es aqe quena de dia
manere que en la florida los an tenido los soldados y los an bendido en españa no
sauiendo su estima Uno en quinientos ducados y otro en aiente doblones que por no
sauer lo que Vali an perdieron mucho en ellos y en la floridaay soldados que an
estade en las minas de Plata que dize y en las se es te uela de los diamanes
conozan destes deyrado puede yn formar ceria dello Un soldado francisco pro
tinaual de la florida que tambien es tan yn ganado de lo dso y otro soldado que
esta en esta corte, en esta tierra ay, mucha comida de mays fresol que es
su comida dellos Ay muchas guindas azuelas Ubaca staña Apilada que
la tienen todo el año ay mançanas mienbro nues muchas capa de todas las
suerte natural mente com en españa, el temple de la tierra es como el desta
y el yngles comforme los yndios andan es tapoblado desde este pueblo a la
el norte Un Rio donde tiene por cierto el dso capitan Vicente gonçales
que Passa la mar del sur porque tratando con los yndios si auia Algun Rio
que passaua Ala, otra mar le rrespondieron que Adelante donde ellos estauan
auia Uno que passaua Ala, otra mar y asi tiene por sin duda que es tan alli los
yngleses. para yr a es te puerto No tiene neçesidad de yr aparecien de
las yndias sino su Viaje derecho porque no Reneguen en bocar canal mi
de reembocar la canal debaxma yarrimarse a la buena Uispa de la mar den
tro de Ourmes. y quando mucho Almedio que es a lo mas que se quede yar
dar Ues de parecer el dso capitan Vicente ecys que se mande juntar el fuerte
de santa Selena con el desan agustin y que con parte de aquella Jente y la
que de Aca fuese se Podria yr ya se es taso Jornada y descubrimiento sin
Reçiuir ningun daño por estar los soldaguera Uenpalicce con gran
Voluntad deyr aella por la noticia que tienen de su Riqueda por lo
Hauer bisto Valgunos por Vista de ojos.

The memorandum of Vicente González had its intended effects. It is not known what the Junta de Puerto Rico suggested, but on October 24 the Council of the Indies recommended that the garrisons in Florida be consolidated at St. Augustine. González should be sent with a frigate loaded with supplies. The king should order artillery to replace the guns Drake had carried off. Finally, an investigation should be undertaken to learn more about the port that González had described in his memorandum. Thus, the immediate need to defend St. Augustine against a new attack by Drake would be met while information useful in planning for the future was accumulated.

The king replied by inquiring as to what new information was in the letters, dated mid-August, that had just been received from Havana. Those letters were restatements of the views of Suarez de Toledo that the English were settled at Bahia de Santa Maria and of other officials at Havana that Drake intended to return to attack the Antilles the following spring. Forwarded to the Junta de Puerto Rico on November 17, the council's suggestions and the letters from Havana seem to have led to a recommendation by the junta that the council's suggestions be implemented. But apparently still uncertain as to the wisdom of consolidating the garrisons, the junta instead recommended that the final decision on that matter be left to Major General Juan de Tejeda, who was being sent with troops and an engineer to provide immediate assistance to the major cities of the Caribbean, including Havana.

As to the matter of searching for the English colony, the king on November 27, 1586, issued to Pedro Menéndez Marqués an order recounting the essence of Vicente González's memorandum concerning the port he had explored earlier and González's theory that the English colony was located on the river that flowed to the "other sea." He instructed Menéndez Marqués to learn as much as he could about this geography, whether the English had begun to utilize the passage to the other sea, where the English were, and what they intended to do. Menéndez Marqués was ordered to report his findings as soon as he could. The search for Roanoke was on.

Despite the instructions to Menéndez Marqués, the search for the English colony was not regarded as a high priority by officials in Madrid. The Spanish were much more involved with and spent far more time after the autumn of 1586 attempting to solve the problems of defending the Caribbean and the convoys. Drake had demonstrated

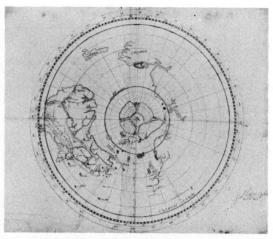

Vicente González presumed that the English colony in North America was located at a strait connecting the Atlantic and Pacific oceans. That theory was supported by English mathematician and astronomer John Dee (left) and others, who maintained that the route could be found near latitude 37 degrees north, the vicinity in which the Roanoke colony was in fact established. Dee included the northwest passage on a map (right) he prepared for Sir Humphrey Gilbert in 1582. Engraving of Dee courtesy Trustees of the British Museum; map from Rare Book Department, Free Library of Philadelphia, Philadelphia, Pennsylvania.

that the forts and militias built up during the previous fifty years were inadequate for defending the major port cities against attacks on the scale he had mounted. New, larger, and more costly forts that would require garrisons for their defense were needed. In addition, the Council of the Indies was pressing for construction of a new fleet of galleons to patrol the Caribbean and escort Spanish convoys. Ships built for that purpose in the early 1580s (to replace another fleet built in 1567) were being used for European naval operations and would likely be drawn into the Armada, the great fleet being prepared at Lisbon to attack England. Apart from seeking long-term solutions to the weakened military condition of the Spanish Empire in the Caribbean, the Council of the Indies and the Junta de Puerto Rico were obliged to concern themselves with the matter of what to do in the event Drake should indeed sail for the Caribbean in the spring of 1587.

In view of all this, an English settlement somewhere north of Santa Elena was not regarded as very important. Even its possible role as a base from which Drake might strike at the Caribbean was secondary to the problem of defending the major ports and shipping. With so many problems with which to deal in addition to routine administrative and judicial matters, the council and other agencies of the government in Madrid were bound to move slowly, dealing with immediate and pressing needs as quickly as the cumbersome bureaucratic processes of Philip's style of administration allowed. Decisions affecting long-term problems were delayed until enough information was available to allow thoughtful and carefully budgeted action. For example, Major General Tejeda and his engineer, while providing immediate assistance to the major towns, were also preparing a master plan for defenses that could be studied and assessed as to cost.

With this context in mind, it becomes clearer why the Spanish search for the English was not pressed with greater vigor. Additional reasons involved the personalities and interests of the men in Florida entrusted with the search and their lack of means, especially shipping.

Menéndez Marqués did not receive his orders until May 2, 1587. By then it was a fixed belief at Havana and in Florida that the English colony was at Jacán on Chesapeake Bay. Too, it was still believed that the English were planning to attack the Antilles from their base in North America, or possibly after seizing St. Augustine. Captain Juan de Posada reported as much from Florida in December, 1586, emphasizing the danger that the English would capture St. Augustine and use it as a base for oared ships to scout the convoys departing the Bahama Channel. To prevent this, Posada urged that the garrisons be consolidated at St. Augustine.

At about the same time, the governor of Havana and the warden of its fort reported the news from Bayaha, Española, that a French ship had encountered forty English vessels 300 leagues east of Dominica. Exactly when that encounter took place was unclear to the Spanish, but they inferred that the English fleet had taken a course to Florida before reaching Puerto Rico, because no English fleet of that size had been reported in the Caribbean since Drake was there. Havana officials emphasized that they expected this fleet to depart the English base in North America in the spring of 1587 and attack Havana, the need for defense of which they outlined once again. The English settlement was, they declared, at Jacán, according to information they had received from Florida. In all probability this was a much-delayed report of Drake's crossing of the Atlantic. No English fleet of such size is known to have been in the mid-Atlantic during the spring or summer of 1586. But whatever plans the English had for 1587, these letters demonstrate that officials in Florida and Havana continued to view the English settlement in the context of their own immediate military needs.

Suarez de Toledo's guess of June, 1586, that the English colony lay in the Chesapeake Bay area, reinforced with information received from sources such as the Jamaican depositions and men captured by Grenville off Bermuda but released in the Azores, had reached Florida and was being fed back to Havana as fact. Perhaps the clearest statement of this belief was in a letter from the warden of the fort at Havana to the president of the House of Trade in Seville. Dated March 22, 1587, it replied to the president's request for verification of the incomplete information available in Seville in September, 1586. The warden wrote that, after asking Menéndez Marqués and Gutierre de Miranda for their news and receiving their replies, he could state that the English viscount who had been at Puerto Rico and Española gathering livestock and had passed the Florida ports in September, 1585, had established a settlement at Jacán, 150 leagues beyond Santa Elena. He noted again the taking of slaves and equipment suitable for a settlement during Drake's raid and the reports of slaves who escaped from Drake at St. Augustine and concluded that these people and equipment were intended for the colony. Menéndez Marqués had advised the warden that, because there was no ship in Florida suitable for the voyage, he could not dispatch a scouting party, but he hoped to do so shortly in order to obtain more certain information. The letter concluded with the observation that the English were probably due west of Bermuda and that their settlement was capable of attacking the Caribbean. Even if they were not there, nothing would be lost by being watchful. Similar information, giving the latitude of Jacán (38 degrees north), was reported in early April by the governor and treasury officials at Havana. This information had it that Drake would return in July, 1587, or such was the confession of a spy Drake had left at Cartagena.

Officials at Havana fitted together the available evidence to show that Grenville, after collecting livestock in the Antilles, had gone north along the Florida coast, made a settlement, and captured a ship from Santo Domingo off Bermuda after leaving his colony. The colony's location was uncertain, but the officials at Havana believed it was at Jacán. They were convinced that Drake or some other Englishman was already there, or would arrive there shortly, to use the post as a staging base for another large-scale raid in the Caribbean.

From English sources it is known that the Spanish were correct in their general belief that an English North American settlement was part of a larger, if very loosely coordinated, plan of naval warfare against the Spanish Caribbean. What the officials at Havana could not know was that Drake had been ordered to attack shipping off the Iberian peninsula and at Cadiz in the spring of 1587 in an effort to break up Spanish preparations for an invasion of England. Drake's renewed attack in the Caribbean did not come in the summer of 1587.

IV. The Search in Florida for the English, 1587-1589

While officials throughout the Caribbean, and especially at Havana, were waiting anxiously to see what would happen in the spring and summer of 1587, Pedro Menéndez Marqués received his order to find out if the English had settled on the coast of Florida and if there was a "strait, as they say there is" to the other sea. Using the frigate that had brought this order from Spain and two barks belonging to the St. Augustine settlement, he set out on May 7, stopping first at Santa Elena to deliver supplies received by ship from Spain. From there he coasted up to about 37 degrees north latitude, "very near Jacán." Apparently putting into some of the estuaries north of Santa Elena, he reported that there was no knowledge of any corsair. He was unable to enter Jacán because on the day he attempted to do so a storm blew up—a storm so strong that it blew his ships to the Bahamas without a "span of sail" on their masts. In the Bahamas he lost one of his barks but saved the crew. Realizing that he was too far south, and having business in Havana, he set a course for that port, arriving on June 19.

In reporting his voyage to the House of Trade, Menéndez Marqués noted that the coast just before Bahia de Santa Maria had three bad shoals that extended far to sea. Elsewhere, however, he found the coast better than between Cape Canaveral and Santa Elena. He had seen many good ports. He intended, he wrote, to sail again later in May or early in June in 1588 and to go better prepared. After asking for permission to explore the coast as far as the Island of St. John (Newfoundland) and then return directly to Spain to report, he concluded his comments with the observation that it was imperative to learn about that coast because "what I saw of it is very different from what the chart shows."[4] Twenty-two years later the pilot Antonio González was to make a similar observation. Spanish lack of interest since the 1520s in the coast north of Winyah Bay was reflected in their charts.

Menéndez Marqués's report to the king has not survived, so it is not known whether it gave more details than the letter just described.

It would be especially helpful to know if the three shoals Menéndez Marqués mentioned in the letter were the three great capes—Fear, Lookout, and Hatteras—or the three bars marking the entrances through the Outer Banks, as some modern scholars have suggested. If the latter were meant, did Menéndez Marqués attempt to explore them and simply miss meeting with Indians who could have told him about the English colony? Or did he pass by the bars at sea, intent on making Bahia de Santa Maria, where he expected to find the English and the strait that Vicente González believed would be found there? The latter seems likely, because Menéndez Marqués's friends at Havana were careful to comment on his zeal to continue seeking out the English and his misfortune in having been driven from the coast by the storm.

His exploration completed for 1587, Menéndez Marqués turned to other matters. The payroll for Florida had arrived from Mexico. There were purchases to make and contracts to arrange for the future supply of the colony. In addition, Menéndez Marqués acquired a ship for the colony's use. Father Luis Gerónimo de Oré points out that the ship was for the voyage to be made in 1588 in search of the English and for Menéndez Marqués's return to Spain. Because Major General Tejeda was in Havana at that time, Menéndez Marqués conferred with him on the question of consolidating the Florida garrisons at St. Augustine and probably about building more permanent fortifications there. They agreed that the troops at Santa Elena would be removed to St. Augustine. Over protests from the lieutenant governor at Santa Elena, Gutierre de Miranda, this was done after Menéndez Marqués returned to Florida in July.

For the next ten months very little effort seems to have been expended to locate the English colony, if available documentation is any indication. At this time, however, Richard Hakluyt, the younger, was publishing the first information about the Roanoke colony. An indication of this is found in the order sent by Philip II's secretary for military affairs to the Junta de Puerto Rico in May, 1587. It instructed the junta to consider the possible importance of the colony the "English Viscount" was "rumored" to have established in Florida, and it noted that reports that he intended to change its location did not necessarily mean he was going to abandon it but rather suggested that he was intent on improving its position.

Exactly how the Spanish learned of Ralegh's and John White's plan to create a new colony on Chesapeake Bay is unknown, but circumstantial evidence points to two books Hakluyt published in 1586 and 1587. The first was Martin Basanier's edition of René de Laudonnière's *L'histoire notable de la Floride,* published at Paris in 1586. In his dedicatory letter Basanier wrote of two voyages made prior to 1586 and of the colony Grenville had established in "Virginia." The second work was Hakluyt's Paris edition of Peter Martyr's *De orbe novo . . . decades octo,* the dedication of which, dated February, 1587, referred to the colony Ralegh was preparing, stated that the expedition was to examine areas not previously explored, and asked Ralegh to find the strait that was the door to China. Furthermore, Hakluyt set forth an English claim to all of America north of 36 degrees north latitude. So far as is known, this book was not available for sale until the summer of 1587, yet the Spanish must have heard about the dedication before that time and combined the information it contained with what they already knew and with Basanier's dedication to conclude that the English intended to move the Grenville colony.

In fact, Ralegh and White planned an entirely separate colony, on the assumption that the Roanoke colony still existed. It is notable that Hakluyt's dedication to the 1587 edition of Peter Martyr suggested a southern limit (36 degrees north) for the quest for the way to the East and reinforced the notion that the English planned to lodge themselves on the strait that Vicente González had said was at about that latitude.

What the Junta de Puerto Rico thought about this new rumor or about Menéndez Marqués's report of his voyage is not known. That document would have been received in Madrid in early October. Apparently an order was dispatched almost at once, or had been dispatched before the report arrived, advising Menéndez Marqués to expect detailed orders from the duke of Medina Sidonia for a voyage up the coast as far as Newfoundland. Menéndez Marqués would receive these orders by mid-May, 1588.

While this instruction made its way across the Atlantic, the king and his councils were considering the engineer's reports on how best to fortify the Caribbean ports. Rumor reaching the Venetian ambassador at Madrid in December, 1587, had it that the king was thinking of building three or four forts in Florida. At least two designs for a fort at St. Augustine were discussed. Perhaps the Venetian ambassador had heard about projects such as those of Vicente González and the Council of the Indies, noted above. On the basis of available documentation, it seems unlikely that the Spanish were already planning to replace the English colony with one of their own. More likely is the possibility that persons at court were talking about a new initiative at Bahia de Santa Maria to tap the wealth that González had reported. In any event, the Junta de Puerto Rico decided in April, 1588, to suspend consideration of the fortification of Florida, except for St. Augustine, until Pedro Menéndez Marqués was on hand to advise it as to what was needed. Given the timetable for his voyage to Newfoundland, that would be in the autumn of 1588 at the earliest.

In Florida, Menéndez Marqués spent the winter of 1587-1588 consolidating his garrison, rebuilding St. Augustine, and waiting for the duke of Medina Sidonia's orders. Two ships were prepared. When the duke's orders failed to arrive by way of a ship that entered St. Augustine harbor from Havana on May 24, Menéndez Marqués decided to take matters into his own hands. Vicente González, once again in Florida, was commissioned to take one of the two ships and a crew of thirty men up the coast to 39 degrees north latitude. Wherever he stopped, he was to take careful latitude readings, soundings, and otherwise map the coast, especially at Bahia de Santa Maria. Once there, he was to attempt to contact Don Luis de Velasco, the Indian who had turned against the Jesuits in 1570. It was hoped that Don Luis would have news of the English and information about a possible strait leading to the southern sea. González could expect to find the English settlement on the shore of that strait. Should the duke of Medina Sidonia's orders arrive after González had sailed, they would be forwarded to him by way of the second ship, probably under Menéndez Marqués's personal command. González departed on June 7. A few weeks later Menéndez Marqués sailed to Havana to see if the duke's orders had arrived there and to take care of business.

The only sources for the voyage of 1588 are Father Luis Gerónimo de Oré's narrative published ca. 1617 as part of a general history of missions in Florida and several fragmentary reports by Juan Menéndez Marqués, Pedro's nephew and the sergeant major of the St. Augustine garrison in 1588. González's report has not been found.

According to Oré, González made port at Santa Elena and Cayagua and at a point beyond the Cape of San Roman, which was either North

Island by Winyah Bay or, more likely, present-day Cape Fear. At the latter landing point, González found that the interpreters accompanying him could no longer understand the Indian languages, an indication that he had entered the Algonquian-speaking areas of modern North Carolina. Continuing up the coast, his ship passed Cabo de Trafalgar, Cabo de San Juan [sic], and two unnamed harbors. The identities of these coastal features are uncertain, but one of the capes was Cape Hatteras and the two harbors were probably the inlets the English called Port Ferdinando and Trinity Harbor. There is no indication that González attempted to enter either; his instructions directed him to proceed to Bahia de Santa Maria, which he did. He entered the bay during the third week of June.

Exploration of the bay took no more than a week. González and his party explored the west side of the Chesapeake, as well as the Eastern Shore of the upper part of the bay. No Indians were encountered until the explorers were north of the Potomac River. For an unstated reason, the Spanish seized one of them. The same thing happened with Indians who appeared in the vicinity of the York River when the explorers returned to the mouth of the bay. What, if anything, was learned from these captives is not stated by Oré, who did, however, indicate that González and his pilot carried out their instructions, taking latitudes and carefully describing the parts of the bay they visited. It was probably evident to González and his party that the English were not to be found along the shores of Chesapeake Bay, and it may have been evident that the supposed strait was not there. A portage over the mountains visible from the vicinity of the Potomac remained a possibility, but no stream navigable by a boat larger than a canoe was found at the head of the bay.

Having completed his reconnaissance of Bahia de Santa Maria and having found nothing, González on June 29 set a course to the south, evidently intending to return directly to St. Augustine without further exploration. That night and the following day he sailed southward with a strong west wind, which probably caused him to take long reaches away from and then toward shore. This zigzag course and a steadily rising wind threatened to carry him well offshore by the evening of June 30. To avoid the experience of Menéndez Marqués the previous spring, González ordered the sails and mast be taken down and the oars run out. His crew rowed for shore. Either that evening or the following morning the ship entered a shallow inlet at latitude 35.5 degrees north, according to Oré. This appears to have been Port Ferdinando. About three nautical miles to the north there was a second inlet (Port Lane), which appeared to be deeper. To the south of the first inlet, at low tide, the bay was quite shallow. To the north, in Roanoke Sound, the Spanish observed a thickly wooded "arm" of what they thought was the mainland. In fact, this was Roanoke Island. Looking around the part of the bay they had entered, the Spanish observed a slipway for small boats, as well as English barrels set into the sand as casings for wells. These objects, along with other debris, indicated that a large number of people had been there. Accident, not deliberate search, had finally revealed to the Spanish the site of the English colony.

After spending the day of July 1 at Port Ferdinando and taking a latitude reading, the Spanish sailed on. They retraced their route down the coast, finally putting in for supplies at present-day Cumberland Island, Georgia. There the Franciscans maintained a mission, at which Indians supplied them with food. From there the Spanish sailed to St. Augustine, arriving about mid-July.

At about the same time, Menéndez Marqués wrote to the king from Havana recounting his preparations for the voyage, the failure of the duke of Medina Sidonia's orders to arrive when promised, and the fact that Vicente González was exploring and had probably returned to St. Augustine by then. Promising to prepare a report on González's voyage once he was back in St. Augustine, Menéndez Marqués then passed along some information obtained from a seaman, Carlos Morera, who claimed that in 1586 he had been in London when a friend arrived aboard another ship and reported that the English were established at 43 degrees north latitude. There was no known English settlement at that latitude in 1585 or 1586. Morera may have heard enough about the English colony to provide him with some talking material, which he probably attempted to parley into a favor by representing it as new information. Menéndez Marqués seems not to have put much stock in this report.

More reliable than Morera's information was news from Pedro de Arana, the royal accountant at Havana. He reported that a sailor named Alonso Ruiz and an unnamed Portuguese pilot had told him about the activities during 1587 of William Irish, a captain dispatched by Sir George Carey, governor of the Isle of Wight. Irish had had several ships, and while off Cuba had intercepted a number of Spanish vessels, including the ship on which Ruiz was a seaman. Following these activities, Irish sailed up the coast of Florida to 37 degrees north and Bahia de Santa Maria, where the English took on water. There they saw "signs of horned cattle with a branded mule," which Arana thought were indications of where the English had their settlement.[5] Arana had also learned that the Indians were not especially friendly to the English and that Drake had taken away the colony. He seems not to have known that the settlement removed by Drake had been replaced with a small garrison left by Grenville when he visited Roanoke to resupply his colony but found it gone. From Bahia de Santa Maria, Irish had sailed to Newfoundland and thence to Ireland and England. Ruiz had obtained his freedom after a few months and had crossed to France, whence he made his way to San Lucar. There he sailed aboard a ship that was run aground near Havana by its crew as it fled from English corsairs.

Ruiz's report did not tell the Spanish anything new about the location of the English colony and may have been distorted by Arana's assumption that the bay Irish entered was Bahia de Santa Maria. On the other hand, Ruiz's news that livestock was roaming loose without there being any sign of the settlers indicated that at the time of Irish's visit the site had been abandoned. Historian David Beers Quinn suggests that Irish could have visited the Roanoke site prior to the arrival of Governor John White and his colonists on August 1, or even the winter settlement of Chesapeake Bay, about which Quinn has written, "we know so little." Certainly, Irish had departed Puerto Rico by the end of June, and a month was more than ample time in which to sail up to Roanoke or Chesapeake Bay. It is less likely that Irish was at the Roanoke site in the autumn. John White left Roanoke Island on September 6 to return to England. The colonists are unlikely to have moved from the island to their intended destination on Chesapeake Bay before the end of that month, which would have put Irish's return to England well into the autumn, a period known to all seamen as stormy and unsuitable for voyages. It appears, then, that Ruiz probably was reporting evidence of the 1586 colony, which had consisted of only eighteen men.

Menéndez Marqués's and Arana's letters were carried by a convoy that departed Havana on August 11 and arrived in Spain in late September. Perhaps because the duke of Medina Sidonia had never sent orders for the exploration; or perhaps because the king had expected Menéndez Marqués to come to Spain that autumn after a careful exploration of the coast as far as Newfoundland, as Menéndez

51

Marqués himself had suggested; or perhaps because the officials in Madrid were growing anxious to know the location of the English colony and were tired of delays caused by Menéndez Marqués's evidently lukewarm interest in the matter—on October 19, 1588, the king signed an order for Menéndez Marqués to explore the coast of Florida as far as Bahia de Santa Maria in search of the English colony and then return to Spain to report. Gutierre de Miranda, who had gone to Spain in the spring of 1588 after Santa Elena was evacuated, would replace Menéndez Marqués as governor of Florida. Miranda had been in Madrid since at least August, presenting his merits-and-services petition before the Council of the Indies and asking for a suitable reward for his work in Florida. He now received his reward, and Menéndez Marqués received permission to return to Spain—permission he had been seeking since 1580.

About the time that the king's order would have reached Menéndez Marqués, had he been in Florida, Pedro de Arana had a stroke of good luck. Pedro Diaz, an experienced pilot who had been to the Straits of Magellan in 1581-1582 when the Spanish established forts there, as well as to many other places in the Atlantic and Caribbean, arrived in Havana and told his story. He had been aboard Alonso Corniele's ship in 1585 when it was captured by Grenville east of Bermuda. But unlike most of the rest of the crew, which had been released at Flores in the Azores, Diaz had been kept prisoner at Plymouth and employed as a pilot. On the last such occasion, in 1587, Diaz's ship encountered a French privateer off Madeira Island. The French captured the English ship and took Diaz with them to the Cape Verde Islands, where he managed to escape, eventually making his way to Cartagena de Indias (Colombia) and thence to Havana. Diaz was able to give a nearly complete account of the English colonizing effort, an account that David Quinn rightly calls "the most important documentary addition to the history of the Roanoke voyages to be made for many years."[6]

Diaz reported that in 1585 Grenville had been in Puerto Rico and La Isabela, Española, gathering cattle, horses, and hogs for the Florida settlement. After leaving the animals and 100 men at the site, he sailed for England, encountering and capturing Corniele's ship off Bermuda. After touching at Flores, Grenville sailed straight to England, arriving at Plymouth on November 26, 1585. From there he went to London, meanwhile confining Diaz and other prisoners to his estate at Bideford, near Barnstaple. Returning to Plymouth at an unspecified date, he prepared six ships, one of 150 tons and the rest in the 60- to 100-ton range. He then assembled 400 seamen and soldiers and supplies for one year.

This 1586 expedition sailed on May 2, making first for Finisterre. There it captured two ships of a group of fourteen making for France and Flanders and sent them to England with prize crews. Sailing farther south, the English encountered and captured a Flemish flyboat, which Grenville kept with him because it was a good sailer and drew little water. The fleet then put into Porto Santo Island in the Madeira group in an effort to obtain water. The Portuguese residents successfully resisted. With this episode Grenville concluded his European privateering, which probably had paid the costs of the voyage, and sailed directly to his colony.

The next passage in Arana's summary of Diaz's testimony is written in almost cryptic Spanish. In his transcription, David Beers Quinn improved upon Irene A. Wright's early translation, but neither version gives the real meaning of the passage, which is a commentary on the commonly held opinion that the English had settled at Bahia de Santa Maria. Arana took pains to demonstrate that this was not true. Edited to make this meaning clear, the passage reads as follows:

He continued his voyage to Florida to where he had left the people, which is at the latitude of 36¼ degrees, [a place] that falls well away from the Bahia de Santa Maria [which is] to the northeast; [that is, the settlement is at a place from whence it is] about 30 leagues to the Cabo de San Juan, [that is,] from where the coast of it [Cabo de San Juan] runs north-south for twelve leagues. [That is] where the settlement is. [It] is an island very close to the mainland that must be about six leagues long. It is possible to pass on foot between the island and the mainland.[7]

The Cabo de San Juan mentioned here is present-day Cape Charles, which is on the north side of the entrance into Chesapeake Bay. It is not clear why Diaz went on to specify that the 30-league distance was to be calculated from the part of the coast north of Cape Charles that ran north-south for a dozen leagues, but it probably would be if a copy of the commonly used Spanish sea chart of that period were available. Nor is it clear what league Diaz was using. The standard Spanish nautical league of the period was 3.1998 modern nautical miles, giving a distance to the eastern shore of Cape Charles of about 96 nautical miles, which is fairly close to the distance from Port Ferdinando. Too, Diaz was estimating in round numbers, not giving an exact distance. However, applying the conversion of 3.1998 nautical miles to the league to Diaz's length for Roanoke Island yields a length of about 19 nautical miles, whereas the island is actually about 10 nautical miles long.

Grenville found the island deserted except for the bodies of one Englishman and one Indian, both of whom had been hanged. Three natives were eventually captured, but two escaped as they were being taken to the ships. The remaining prisoner told Grenville that the colonists and the island Indians had been in a battle with the mainland Indians, in which battle four Englishmen died. The colonists had been forced to disperse because of the failure of the island's soil to produce enough food. Drake had come and taken them away. Although Diaz was not allowed ashore, he was able to report that the colony's fort was by the water and consisted of nothing but timbers having "no great strength."[8]

Grenville landed eighteen men, four pieces of iron artillery, and enough supplies to last for a year. Englishmen named Cofar (Coffin?) and Chapman were left in charge. Fourteen days after arriving, the fleet sailed.

The English were convinced, Diaz said, that there was gold on the mainland, as well as a waterway from the Atlantic to the Pacific oceans nearby. They intended to establish themselves firmly wherever they might find wealth. This confirmed what Hakluyt's dedication of 1587 had already demonstrated: that Grenville and Ralegh accepted the same geographic theory as did the French, Menéndez de Avilés, and Vicente González.

After leaving North America the fleet sailed to the Azores and then to Newfoundland for fish before returning to the Azores to raid shipping. That accomplished, the English returned home.

Once again Grenville went to London to recruit men and women for his colony. According to Diaz, Grenville gathered some 210 people and sent them abroad with Simon Fernandes, "a great pilot and the person who induced them to settle there." This expedition sailed from London in March, 1587. It is known as John White's colony, the third in the series and the one Ralegh intended to establish on the Chesapeake as a settlement separate from Grenville's Roanoke Island post.

Evidently from later reports rather than firsthand knowledge, Diaz learned that none of the eighteen men Grenville had left on the island were found, nor was there any trace of them. The new settlers were deposited, and the ships returned to England. Diaz did not know that this happened because the shipmasters, concerned about the weather (they had already encountered one storm while off the Outer Banks), were impatient to sail and thus were unwilling to carry the colonists to Chesapeake Bay.

When the ships were back in England, Grenville equipped two vessels (the *Brave* and the *Roe*) to carry supplies to the new colony. Seven men and four women were also sent. Diaz was the pilot of one ship, and a Captain Artefas (Amadas?) was put in command of the expedition. Off Mareira, Diaz's ship was taken by French privateers, as previously noted. After telling the rest of his story (related above), Diaz concluded his deposition.

Arana's covering letters fairly gloat over his discovery. He understood, he told Philip II, that the king had been very insistent on learning where the English were (which probably means Arana had heard of earlier orders to Menéndez Marqués as well as that of October, 1588). Menéndez Marqués had made some efforts "of little moment" and had not obtained the information the king sought. Arana now forwarded this information in the form of Diaz's report. Writing to the king's secretary, Juan de Ibarra, Arana was less restrained, saying, "with the unfailing desire in which I live to succeed in serving his majesty, . . . [I] have made a relation of the place where the English are settling on the Florida coast. From my report the truth will be learnt, very different, indeed, from the reports which have already been sent to his majesty, all of which have been intended to serve the ends of certain individuals without involving them in risks of any kind."[9] Not surprisingly, Arana went on to ask that he be transferred to a post of greater importance, one in which serving the king would not cost him money (a standard complaint of the king's officials).

Arana was clearly critical of Menéndez Marqués, who indeed had done little to seek out the English. As has been noted, in 1587 Menéndez Marqués let bad weather serve as an excuse to postpone further exploration until the following spring. While in 1588 he had been more forceful, his instructions to Vicente González did not direct him to undertake a port-by-port search for the English. Rather, González was directed to go to Bahia de Santa Maria to verify a report that González himself had made to the king. Only by force of circumstances (weather again) had González stumbled upon the true location of the English colony, a fact that may not have been known to Arana when he wrote his letter on March 26, 1589.

Whether Menéndez Marqués can justly be accused of making reports that served his own ends is a moot point. He certainly had reasons for wanting to postpone action during a time when the St. Augustine colony was in great need of his full attention. Furthermore, it is clear that the colony had too little shipping and supplies to justify consigning even one frigate and a tender to a search in and out of harbors with entrances made treacherous by shifting sandbars. Only direct royal orders seem to have overridden Menéndez Marqués's tendency to use his resources to address the problem at hand, especially because he professed to believe that his colony was in danger of a new attack by Francis Drake. Too, the documentary record does not indicate that he had a personal interest in Bahia de Santa Maria. Rather, it suggests that his own economic interests were in St. Augustine and the supply of its garrison. González, on the other hand, was clearly guilty as charged, if he was one of the "certain individuals" Arana had in mind. But Arana may have been referring to other parties, men whose interests in Bahia de Santa Maria are now unknown.

Whatever the intent behind Arana's veiled criticism, the information he forwarded with Pedro Diaz to Seville gave the Spanish confirmation of information that Vicente González and Pedro Menéndez Marqués were also attempting to carry to Spain in that spring of 1589. They had originally sailed for Spain on October 28, 1588, and had come within sight of Bermuda, according to Juan Menéndez Marqués, when a storm forced them to run southeast for the Antilles. They seem to have entered the Caribbean from the east and then sailed along south of Puerto Rico and Española. Failing to find Santo Domingo because of bad weather, they sailed on to La Yaguana, located near the present site of Port-au-Prince, Haiti. By then, the voyagers were in great distress. Bad weather continued to dog them when they attempted to sail on to Spain by taking the Windward Passage. Unable to sail around Cabo San Nicolas because of the weather, they set a course that took them along the northern coast of Cuba to Havana.

It is not known when the Florida voyagers reached Havana, but they were there in April, 1589. In a later letter Menéndez Marqués commented that during his visit to Havana in April no news had been received of the voyage of Major General Tejeda and the men and equipment he was bringing to the Caribbean to begin building more permanent fortifications at Puerto Rico, Santo Domingo, and Havana. It may well be that Menéndez Marqués was in Havana when Arana wrote his letter of March 26.

Having transacted some business on behalf of the Florida garrison, Menéndez Marqués and his party returned to St. Augustine. They may have arrived by May 3, when certain supplies from Cuba were sold to the treasury. In any case, Menéndez Marqués and his companions sailed again for Spain on May 19, 1589. This time the weather was favorable, and they made a crossing that placed them at San Lucar de Barameda in early July and at Seville on the morning of July 5.

V. Action Delayed, 1589-1609

The arrival of Pedro Menéndez Marqués and his party at Seville on July 5 opened what proved to be the final chapter in the story of Spanish concern about the Roanoke Island colonies. Little is known about this part of the story, but what is known suggests that the immediate matter of defending the Caribbean and St. Augustine and a complicated series of problems within the government of Spanish Florida caused the postponement during the 1590s of any project to expel the English from their base at Roanoke Island. When the idea came up again in 1600, it was as part of a scheme to remove the English and then establish a base from which the Spanish could explore the interior of North America in order to find the mines that Captain Juan Pardo's men had reported. But that plan, too, came to nothing. After an incident in 1604 revealed that some Englishmen thought the Roanoke Island colony still existed, the Spanish went in search of it but got no further than Cape Fear. Thereafter, Spanish searches for an English colony centered on the Jamestown, Virginia, colony, which the Spanish correctly took to be the long-delayed movement of the settlers to Bahia de Santa Maria that had first been rumored in 1587. The search for and surveillance of Jamestown that began in 1609 is, however, a story that lies outside the scope of this study.

Menéndez Marqués did not leave Seville for Madrid until after July 24, 1589, and he arrived at court by the end of July. While there, he and Juan Menéndez Marqués, his nephew, were questioned by the Council of the Indies concerning Bahia de Santa Maria and the information that Vicente González's voyage and Pedro Diaz had supplied concerning the location of the English colony. The king's secretaries, Juan de Idiaquez and Juan de Ibarra, also discussed these issues with the men from Florida. Once that had been done, Juan Menéndez Marqués was sent back to Seville. The duke of Medina Sidonia soon set him to work at San Lucar preparing two new *galizabras* for a transatlantic voyage.

As Juan Menéndez Marqués later told the story, when Pedro Menéndez Marqués arrived at San Lucar, probably in April, he told Juan that it had been decided that he, Pedro, was to take four storeships, a number of men, and a large quantity of supplies to Florida by way of Havana. There he would obtain the Cuban galleys and such other ships as he thought suitable for entering the shallow bay where the English were established. With those ships in his company, Menéndez de Avilés was to go to St. Augustine, disembark the new soldiers, and replace them with an equal number of experienced men from the St. Augustine garrison. His expedition was then to proceed to the location of the enemy's fort and settlement and attempt to destroy it. The storeships were to go ahead to Bahia de Santa Maria. Once Pedro Menéndez Marqués had taken care of the English, he was to join the storeships, explore the bay, and select a site for a fort, where as many as 300 men were to be left under a warden—none other than Juan Menéndez Marqués. The latter's orders were to take the first opportunity to march inland with a goodly part of his force and determine what the land was like and what minerals and gems might be found there. Juan Pardo's mines still echoed in men's minds.

This story was plausible in that many parts of the project it described had been suggested earlier. Vicente González's memorandum of September, 1586, provided the general outline. The use of galleys had been suggested in 1587 by the factor of Florida, Captain Rodrigo de Junco, who thought their size and ability to enter and leave shallow waters ideal for exploration and for dealing with any enemy ships encountered. Finally, the need for more men had been a theme in letters from Florida for more than a decade. The scale of the proposed expedition was consistent with what the Spanish knew about the size of the English colony.

Plausible as this story was, it was but a deception agreed upon by Philip II and his trusted advisers. In fact, Menéndez Marqués had secret orders to take the two *galizabras* and make a dash to the Isthmus of Panama to obtain the king's revenues from Peru and take them back to Spain without making the customary port stops on the return voyage. This extraordinary and dangerous method of returning the king's treasure was resorted to because the Tierra Firme (Spanish Main) convoy was not expected to sail promptly in the spring of 1590 or return to Spain until 1591. Deception as to the true mission of Menéndez Marqués would protect these two small, lightly armed ships from interception by the fleet the English were reported to be preparing to intercept the returning Spanish convoys in European waters. Philip II needed the money too much to leave in doubt either its prompt delivery to Spain or its safety in transit.

True to his orders, Pedro Menéndez Marqués sailed on May 16 from Cadiz directly to Cartagena de Indias. He departed Cartagena on July 7 and was in Havana on July 20. The *galizabras* tied up at Viana, Portugal, at the end of August. The king's treasure was safe for another year.

That autumn the Council of the Indies received confirmation of the rumors and reports that had led to the extraordinary voyage of Menéndez Marqués. The mail sent from Havana in late August contained a number of letters and depositions taken from seamen who had been aboard a ship called *El Buen Jesus* that was captured by the English earlier in the summer of 1590. Testifying at Havana in mid-August, these men said that they understood that the English had a settlement at a certain harbor in Florida. Forty ships had departed England in the spring of 1590 for the Caribbean. All intended to rendezvous at the colony. Four of these forty were said to be carrying women to the colony. The English planned to sail from their settlement in the late summer of 1590 to attempt to intercept the Tierra Firme convoy and then in 1591 to assemble 150 ships at their base for an attack on Havana. The group of five English ships that had captured *El Buen Jesus* had carried a "governor" for the colony and planned to winter at the settlement.

From a letter written by the commander of the Tierra Firme convoy, the Council of the Indies learned what it knew by the time the letter was received in Madrid and reviewed, along with other news, in a memorandum the council sent to the king on November 8: that the English had sent two squadrons to patrol off the Azores and the capes of southern Portugal. Both squadrons were to attempt to intercept one or more of the convoys. To further that end, the English had stationed a ship east of Havana to gather the latest information on the movement of the convoys toward the Azores in the late summer. In view of these dangers, the lateness of the Tierra Firme convoy's arrival at Havana (in July), the poor physical and military condition of the ships in the convoy, and the small number of royal warships sent to escort it from Havana, the Spanish commanders of the convoy and escort force decided to winter at Havana.

Confirmation that the English were still in Florida and that a governor for their settlement was aboard one of the ships that had been in the Antilles came from letters written by the governor of Puerto Rico in May and, via a duplicate of a letter that the English intercepted, in September. In the latter the Spanish governor complained that the reason so many privateers were in his area of the Caribbean at all seasons of the year instead of just the spring was that they were utilizing Florida as a base and wintering port.

In fact, John White was aboard the *Hopewell* when it passed through the Antilles. He was governor of Ralegh's colony. As many as four of the seven ships that had been given permission to leave England that spring, or had sailed before Queen Elizabeth I embargoed all voyages because of the threat of a new Spanish naval attack, were intended to visit, if not winter at, Roanoke. But forty ships had not been allowed out of England. Whatever plans there may have been to send out settlers, including women, it is known from English sources that only John White and, probably, the supplies that could be fitted into the 80-ton capacity of the *Moonlight* and the 20- to 30-ton capacity of the pinnace *Conclude* were actually sent. As to English plans for 1591, the report of 150 ships appears to have been propaganda intended to frighten the Spanish and divert resources from any expeditions against England. Nevertheless, the English were established on the North American coast, and their base was a potential threat to the security of the Antilles and the ships moving through the Bahama Channel on the way to Spain.

Somewhat more reliable information about English plans for 1591 had reached the council from the duke of Medina Sidonia. He had interviewed seamen from various ships from the Caribbean and Brazil who had been captured by the English and held briefly in England. The seamen reported that Drake was arming twenty galleons for an attack on Havana, a report the council found believable because the English were not then engaged in a naval war that would keep them occupied in Europe. The council also accepted as fact reports from the Caribbean that the English were using their North American base for wintering (although there is no information that any English ship ever did).

The council concluded that sending soldiers, as had been done with Major General Juan de Tejeda and as was being planned for 1591, would not be enough defense for the Caribbean. Rather, a fleet should be sent there, not kept in European waters as originally planned. Finally, as a postscript, the council noted reports that the English were preparing an expedition to sail to the Pacific.

In a note written on the cover of this memorandum of November 8, 1590, one of the king's secretaries declared: "In regards the English who have settled in Florida, when it can be done, expelling them from there will be looked at in all the respects that ought to be considered."[10]

It is not known if anything further was done. The man who would have directed any move to expel the English was otherwise occupied. Pedro Menéndez Marqués was sent to the Caribbean in the spring of 1591 to bring home again the king's Peruvian revenues in the *galizabras.* He sailed on May 9 and had the funds loaded and his ships once again at Cartagena de Indias ready to sail for Spain by July 18. But he did not sail for Havana until September 7 and did not attempt to leave that port until November. Bad weather prevented him from clearing the Bahama Channel until December. The money reached Spain on January 19, 1592.

Rumors of a large English presence in North America continued to circulate in Europe, even though John White had returned to England in the autumn of 1590 with the news that the Roanoke colony had disappeared, leaving only the word "CROATOAN" carved on a post to the right of the entrance to the wooden palisade, some metal debris inside the fort, and five chests discovered in the fort's ditch partially buried but plundered.

In Florida any possibility of locally initiated action against the English was lost because of problems of government and supply that were not resolved until 1597. In addition, the colony became internally divided between those who wanted to move the settlement to the area of the Franciscan missions in modern Georgia and those who wanted to leave it where it was at St. Augustine. These troubles began shortly after Gutierre de Miranda arrived in 1590 to take up his duties as governor.

Gutierre de Miranda's martinet-like behavior soon provoked a rebellion among the soldiers. They arrested him and elected one of their number to serve as governor until the king might provide a new governor. Miranda's death in prison and the need to send someone to restore discipline led to the appointment in 1592 of Captain Rodrigo de Junco as governor. But Junco was lost in a shipwreck as he reached

Florida. By then, receipt of the payroll from Mexico had been interrupted for more than two years, as had the sending of supplies from Spain and the Canary Islands. Junco did take some new men and contracted with a Spanish merchant for the supply of the colony, but those actions were inadequate to meet the needs of the garrison at St. Augustine for reinforcements and munitions, much less to equip it to expel the English. An effort in 1593 to obtain supplies from Mexico ended in a complex tangle of problems when the man sent to collect the payroll and buy supplies died there.

In addition to these difficulties of supply and leadership, Florida came under scrutiny in 1593 because its accountant, Bartolome de Arguelles, who was in Spain seeking supplies and assistance, suggested that the garrison be moved north to the bar of Guale. By this Arguelles seems to have meant Altamaha Sound or Doboy Sound (according to the distance specified), although he may have had Sapelo Sound in mind inasmuch as he said that there were located there ports that large ships could enter. Besides better ports—St. Augustine could accept ships of only 40 tons or smaller, Arguelles said—the area of Guale offered better land than the sand and swamps around St. Augustine.

The hand of the Franciscans probably lay behind this recommendation, because they maintained missions in the Guale district and presumably sought the military presence for protection. When Pedro Menéndez Marqués and others were consulted, they recommended that no change be made. Nor did the former governor of Florida approve moving the fort to the head of the Florida Keys, which the Council of the Indies still considered to be an alternative. In short, things should remain as they were, with the immediate problem of sending to Florida replacement and reinforcement troops, along with a governor, taking priority over plans to move the fort. Searching for the English did not even figure in the discussion.

And indeed, during that spring of 1593 Pedro Menéndez Marqués was advising the king how to raise troops for Florida without the men suspecting that that was their destination. The colony had such a bad reputation, Menéndez Marqués noted, that no one would willingly sign up to go there. Instead, each of the frigates scheduled to sail for the Caribbean should have twenty-five extra men put aboard, and the ship Arguelles had brought from Florida, as well as another vessel, should be prepared for the return trip. Once the frigates and those ships were at Dominica, 150 men could be selected from among the soldiers aboard the frigates and sent to Florida. Apparently approving this idea, the king named Menéndez Marqués governor of Florida, explaining in a letter of July 25 how important it was that a man of his experience should go there and reassert royal authority.

Menéndez Marqués objected, saying that he would lose honor by accepting a lesser command after having been commander of the king's fleet. Instead, he suggested, the king should appoint Bartolome de León, one of Menéndez Marqués's kinsmen. Philip II insisted. Menéndez Marqués continued to offer excuses and finally, in September, when the sailing date of the ships was approaching, took to his bed, claiming to be too ill to return to the Caribbean. Apparently he was sick, but he soon recovered when the king granted him additional benefits (*mercedes*) and made it clear through officials of the House of Trade that his mission was to take troops to Puerto Rico and Havana, to exchange some men at Havana for others, and then to proceed to Florida, where he was to remain only long enough to restore order.

Again becoming ill in January, Menéndez Marqués was finally replaced as governor by Captain Domingo Martinez de Avendaño. By then the king had appointed a new set of treasury officials, including Juan Menéndez Marqués as treasurer, and had made arrangements for the supply of Florida. Avendaño was instructed to sail directly to Florida, isolate and arrest the men reported most guilty of leading the rebellion, and, once he had firm control of the garrison, send to Havana for replacements. Dispatched to Havana and Puerto Rico that spring were additional orders that provided for the rotation of some of the soldiers in each garrison. Fifty-four men went to Havana from Puerto Rico, and thirty men were selected at Havana for Florida.

Avendaño sailed from Spain on February 25, 1594. Among the men who went with him was Vicente González. The king commended González to Avendaño with an order to see that he be provided with a post and support appropriate to his long experience and service. Thus the man who could lead the Spanish to Roanoke returned to St. Augustine, but he was never given the opportunity to use his knowledge.

Avendaño quickly took charge of the troops in St. Augustine and arrested the leaders of the rebellion. He then went on an inspection tour to Guale. He displayed great energy and seems to have impressed Indians, Franciscans, and Florida veterans alike. But on the way home he became ill with a "bloody flux," which caused his death on November 25, 1595. Once again, the Spanish in Florida were leaderless, and once again it took more than a year—until June 2, 1597—for a new governor to be appointed and to arrive in St. Augustine.

Governor Gonzalo Méndez Canzo arrived just before the supposedly Christian Indians of the Guale missions revolted against their Franciscan tutors. His campaign against these rebels was swift and, in the eyes of some, brutal. Once order had been restored, the remaining Franciscans began to ask for and then demand military protection for their missions.

Meanwhile, Méndez Canzo became fascinated with reports of Tama, a province located west of the Guale area on the present Georgia coast. Tama was reputed to be not only rich in agricultural potential but also situated near the silver, gold, and diamond mines that Captain Juan Pardo's expedition had discovered. Writing to the king early in 1598, Méndez Canzo proposed that a new Spanish town be founded at Tama and used as a base for additional explorations westward until contact was made with other Spanish explorers he believed were coming eastward from New Mexico. In 1599 the frustrated Franciscans began to send the king written complaints about the location of the garrison and Méndez Canzo's failure to support them.

The government of Philip III, who had become king upon the death of his father on September 13, 1598, responded to Méndez Canzo's proposals concerning Tama with a request for additional detailed information. This request, dated November 9, 1598, did not reach Méndez Canzo until January 18, 1600. The man who had taken Méndez Canzo's request to court and was returning with the king's reply was captured and held for five months by French privateers. He managed to send his dispatches to Puerto Rico, but they were not forwarded until he retrieved them.

Writing on February 28, 1600, in reply to the request for additional information, Méndez Canzo told Philip III that he could forward only the deposition of one Gaspar de Salas, the only man who had been to Tama. Salas had been unable to draw a map, as had been requested. Testimony by others, including two Indian women (probably

Philip III (1578-1621) succeeded to the throne of Spain following the death of his father, Philip II, in September, 1598. He inherited from his father a number of problems connected with Spain's New World empire, and his reign, like that of his father, was characterized by a decline in Spanish power and influence. Engraving from Brown, *The Genesis of the United States*, I, facing p. xviii.

Cherokee) who had been brought from the interior in 1570 when the last of Captain Juan Pardo's garrisons had abandoned the forts built in 1566-1568, confirmed certain details concerning the reputed richness of the area. Nevertheless, the information was sketchy at best.

In making his inquiries, Méndez Canzo had, however, discovered "David Glauid," whose real name was probably Darby Glavin. A deserter from John White's 1587 voyage, this Irishman had been with Grenville to the town the latter had founded at Jacán at latitude 35.5 degrees north. Glavin had been evacuated by Drake and then compelled to go on a second voyage, but he had escaped at Puerto Rico.

Glavin's testimony, and a map he was able to draw of the coast and various rivers, suggested to Méndez Canzo that he had been mistaken in his advocacy of Tama. Instead, he drew up a plan for an expedition against the English colony that Glavin supposed was then at 37 degrees north latitude. (Glavin knew that it was to be moved to Chesapeake Bay.) Méndez Canzo was certain that an expedition of 1,000 men with ships and supplies could deal with the English if they were there. Should they not be there, the expedition could do whatever the king might order. Méndez Canzo apparently did not mean by this that a colony should be established at Bahia de Santa Maria, even though it was situated at a latitude that explorers coming to Florida from New Mexico would have to pass; rather, he seems to have thought that some of the men could be used in the project he mentioned next.

The correct method for exploring the interior as far as New Mexico, he said, was to send 300 soldiers. They could live off the land once in the interior and should follow the route Pardo had taken, which commenced at Santa Elena and would take them to the general area of Tama. Trade goods and various kinds of supplies, including ten horses, were also needed. The leader of the expedition from New Mexico that this force could be expected to meet should be instructed to consult with the leader from Florida and accept his advice concerning which port, fort site, or other destination should be selected. It is not known whether Méndez Canzo meant on the Gulf coast or on the shore of the purported arm of the Pacific that ran north of New Mexico.

Accompanying Méndez Canzo's letter and the depositions of the witnesses previously noted were other letters that argued for the removal of the garrison to the present Georgia coast, where it could better protect the Franciscan missions and where, the king was assured, there were better soils and more favorable prospects for the colony's success. Father Baltasar Lopez, the Franciscan stationed at Cumberland Island, and Alonso de las Alas, a factor, also endorsed a fort at the head of the Florida Keys, a location that would be useful for assisting shipwrecked seamen, for whaling, and for other purposes. A final letter was from Father Blas Montes, the Franciscan superior in Florida, whose principal interest was in obtaining from the king funds to help rebuild the friary following its destruction by fire on March 14, 1599. But Father Montes's remarks suggested more sympathy for those who wanted to move the garrison to the north.

When these suggestions that St. Augustine be abandoned, or at least supplemented by additional settlements, reached Madrid, they provoked Philip III to issue an order dated November 5, 1600, and addressed to the governor of Cuba, Pedro de Valdés. As was customary in such documents, the king recounted the gist of various memorandums and letters he had received (and which may have been removed from the archives of the Council of the Indies for the occasion). They indicated, he wrote, that Florida should be abandoned because the Indians did not want to become Christian and did not produce much in the way of agricultural goods. Moreover, they suggested that the land lacked mineral resources, had no good port on its long coast (that is, none where convoys could find shelter from storms), did not lead to any place of interest to the Spanish, and would not be a threat to the empire if held by another nation. Valdés was to investigate

67

these matters, especially the status of the Indians, the number of Christian conversions among them, the productivity of the soil, the pros and cons of dismantling St. Augustine, and the cost of the province to the royal treasury.

This order reached Havana in August, 1602. On the fourteenth of that month the governor appointed his son, Fernando de Valdés, to go to Florida and investigate. The younger Valdés began his work at St. Augustine on August 31. Eighteen witnesses, selected from the residents of longest term in Florida, the treasury officials, and the Franciscans, were asked to respond to five questions. The first two questions focused on the conversion of the natives and the conquest of the land. The third inquired about resources, both agricultural and mineral. The fourth called for opinions on whether there were better ports than St. Augustine in Florida and what benefits or disadvantages might result from dismantling the St. Augustine garrison and leaving its port for possible occupation by an enemy. The final question dealt with whether there were ports suitable for convoys, where the land of Florida led, and the danger of enemy occupation of strategic places in Florida.

Most witnesses deferred to the Franciscans on the question of whether the missions were successful; agreed that ports as good or better than St. Augustine lay to the north, especially at Zapala (Sapelo Sound), Santa Elena (Port Royal Sound), and Cayagua (Charleston harbor), although they knew little about the coast when questioned in detail; and were generally against abandonment. St. Augustine had been the salvation of more than 500 shipwrecked and storm-tossed voyagers during the previous decade. Most depositions included a good deal of hearsay evidence concerning the richness of the interior that Pardo had visited. On the question of possible enemy occupation, about which most witnesses did not even comment, the few who did repeated the fears of 1586 and 1590 that Francis Drake would seize St. Augustine, if it were abandoned, because of its strategic position relative to the mouth of the Bahama Channel.

Significantly, none of the witnesses expressed any concern about the reputed English presence at Bahia de Santa Maria. In fact, except for Juan de Lara, who had been to Jacán as a youth in 1570, former treasurer Juan Lopez de Avilés, and treasurer Juan Menéndez Marqués, who had been to Jacán in 1588, none of the witnesses even mentioned the northern bay. Menéndez Marqués spoke about it at some length and with enthusiasm as a place worth further investigation, but he did not recommend settlement there.

When the Franciscans were given their opportunity to testify, they presented a picture of success in the mission work but a lack of support from governors past and, especially, present. Not surprisingly, all three friars who testified recommended that the town be shifted to a location in or close to the Guale mission field. Like most of the other witnesses, they expressed no concern about a possible English presence in North America.

Gonzalo Méndez Canzo was not called to testify but wrote his own long letter to the king on the same questions. While acknowledging some success for the missions, he was critical of the Franciscans. He defended himself and his actions as governor against various charges, noted the possibilities for making the soils of St. Augustine yield crops, and boasted of what he had done to increase agricultural production. Reviewing the ports along the coast, he said that none of those between St. Augustine and Santa Elena was of any use—a view shared by the pilots called to testify. The coast northward from Santa Elena to Jacán, on the other hand, was better and should be explored. He then recounted his ideas concerning Tama and how it might be explored and conquered. Méndez Canzo concluded with a defense of St. Augustine as a necessary support for the various villages of Christian Indians that surrounded it and as a refuge for storm-tossed seamen. To save money and to free men for the Tama expedition, he suggested reducing the size of the St. Augustine garrison from 300 to 120 men. Furthermore, he advised that the treasury should be reorganized, eliminating the offices of treasurer and factor and replacing them with a storekeeper. An accountant would still be needed, he noted, along with a governor. He closed with suggestions concerning the support of the Franciscans.

The outcome of this inquiry, grandly mislabeled by a ⌐other writer as the trial of Florida, was that nothing was done to move St. Augustine or to explore the interior. Méndez Canzo was recalled in the autumn of 1602, effective in 1603.

Méndez Canzo's successor as governor, Pedro de Ibarra, was more concerned than his predecessor with possible foreign intrusion into Spanish North America. On one occasion, the 1604 voyage of the *Castor and Pollux* to the present coast of Georgia to trade, he succeeded in capturing the crew of that Franco-English trading ship. From some of the crewmen he learned that the English colony to the north was thought to be there still. That news caused him to send Captain Francisco de Ecija to search for the settlement. For a variety of reasons Ecija got only as far as Cape Fear before turning back to St. Augustine.

These events were reported to the Council of the Indies, which was again considering the question of what sort of fort to build in Florida, and where. Asked for his opinion on the location, Mendez Canzo expressed opposition to St. Augustine, a view that may have helped further postpone action as the council attempted to discover the best policy to follow. Bureaucratic inertia had increased substantially since the death of Philip II in 1598.

In the midst of this indecision came the news that the English were once again planning to colonize in North America. Coming from Spanish diplomats in London, this information was certain. In response, the Spanish attempted via diplomacy to persuade the English to abandon the project and sent orders (the first since 1587) to the governor of Florida to search for the English colony. The orders specifically mentioned Pedro Diaz's testimony of 1589, which gave the location of the settlement.

The English had left Roanoke behind and moved on to the great bay to the north, Bahia de Santa Maria, or Chesapeake Bay. The opportunity to dislodge the English from the east coast of North America and establish a Spanish presence at the bay, so long advocated by a few men who had been there and realized its possibilities, was rapidly slipping from Spain's grasp. But the Spanish could not see that clearly when their first scouting party entered Chesapeake Bay in 1609 and found a large English ship, which was a certain sign that the colonists had arrived in force and had come to stay.

Notes

[1]Lawrence C. Wroth, *The Voyages of Giovanni de Verrazzano, 1524-1528* (New Haven: Yale University Press, 1970), 136.

[2]Irene A. Wright (ed.), *Further English Voyages to Spanish America, 1583-1594* (London: Hakluyt Society, 1951), 173, hereinafter cited as Wright, *Further English Voyages.*

[3]Wright, *Further English Voyages,* 187.

[4]Wright, *Further English Voyages,* 232-233.

[5]Wright, *Further English Voyages,* 234.

[6]David B. Quinn (ed.), *The Roanoke Voyages, 1584-1590* (London: Hakluyt Society, 2 volumes, 1955), II, 786, n. 1.

[7]Archivo General de Indias, Santo Domingo 118.

[8]Wright, *Further English Voyages,* 239.

[9]Archivo General de Indias, Santo Domingo 118.

[10]Consulta of Council of Indies, November 8, 1590, Archivo de Indias, Indiferente General 741.

Suggestions for Additional Reading and Study

The study of Spanish knowledge of and reactions to the Roanoke colonies rests on documentation found in the Archive of the Indies. The most important documents have been edited and translated in David B. Quinn, ed., *The Roanoke Voyages, 1584-1590* (London: Hakluyt Society, 2 volumes, 1955) and in Irene A. Wright, ed., *Further English Voyages to Spanish America, 1583-1594* (London: Hakluyt Society, 1951). Of these collections, Quinn's is by far the most comprehensive, and his introductions to the documents (including English sources) are more informative for the beginning student. He has published some of the same documents, as well as additional ones not available in 1955, in David B. Quinn, ed., *New American World: A Documentary History of North America to 1612* (New York: Arno Press, 5 volumes, 1979). This latter collection is especially useful for Spanish knowledge and reactions in the 1590s and early 1600s. Reproductions of the more important Spanish, French, and English maps, together with a brief narrative, are found in William P. Cumming, R. A. Skelton, and David B. Quinn, *The Discovery of North America* (New York: Heritage Press, 1972).

The standard study of the Spanish presence in Florida to 1574 is Woodbury Lowery, *Spanish Settlements within the Present Limits of the United States* (New York: Putnam, 2 volumes, 1901-1911; reprint edition, 1959). Paul E. Hoffman, "The Chicora Legend," *Florida Historical Quarterly*, 62 (April, 1984), 419-438, traces the Ayllón voyages and their impact on later explorers of the southeast coast. See also Paul E. Hoffman, "New Light on Vicente Gonzalez's 1588 Voyage in Search of Raleigh's English Colonies," *North Carolina Historical Review*, LXIII (April, 1986), 199-223. Eugene Lyon, *The Enterprise of Florida: Pedro Menéndez de Avilés and the Conquest of 1565-1568* (Gainesville: University Presses of Florida, 1976), is the authority on the years 1565-1568. There is no study comparable to either Lowery or Lyon for the post-1574 period, but Maynard Geiger, *The Franciscan Conquest of Florida, 1573-1618* (Washington, D.C.: Catholic University of America, 1937), supplies much of the essential information.

A dated but still useful introduction to Spanish colonial institutions is Clarence Haring, *The Spanish Empire in America* (New York: Harcourt, Brace and World, third edition, 1963). Kenneth R. Andrews, *The Spanish Caribbean: Trade and Plunder, 1530-1630* (New Haven: Yale University Press, 1978), provides a general overview of Caribbean history, including non-Spanish activities. For military conditions prior to Francis Drake's raid of 1586, see

Paul E. Hoffman, *The Spanish Crown and the Defense of the Caribbean, 1535-1585* (Baton Rouge: Louisiana State University Press, 1980). Details of Drake's raid can be found in Wright, *Further English Voyages.*

James Leitch Wright, *Anglo-Spanish Rivalry in North America* (Athens: University of Georgia Press, 1971), provides an overview of the diplomatic as well as the colonial struggle. Selected diplomatic reports are in Quinn, *Roanoke Voyages.* David B. Quinn, "Some Spanish Reactions to Elizabethan Colonial Enterprises," *Transactions of the Royal Historical Society,* fifth series, I (1951), 1-23, is a summary of the topic of this booklet. For additional materials of interest, the student should consult the bibliographies of the works cited here, especially those by David B. Quinn.